The Child and Society

The Process of Socialization

FREDERICK ELKIN
McGill University

RANDOM HOUSE
New York

TO MADGE

Fifth Printing, August 1963

© Copyright, 1960, by Random House, Inc.

Library of Congress Catalog Card Number: 60-16607

Manufactured in the United States of America

The Child and Society

STUDIES IN
SOCIOLOGY

PREFACE

A volume of this size is necessarily limited in the material it can cover. The focus of this study is on socialization in everyday life in modern society. Two types of material especially relevant to socialization are barely touched on: that gathered by anthropologists describing patterns in other societies and that accumulated by psychologists in laboratory experiments and other more precisely controlled situations. Anthropologists have shown the extensive range of behavior children are capable of learning and the many varied techniques employed in child training; psychologists, above all else, have amassed considerable data on the development of children and have held up the ideal of cumulative and organized knowledge.

I should like to express my gratitude to Charles H. Page, editor of this series, for his encouragement and invaluable suggestions on style and content.

CONTENTS

The Child and Society

1 SOCIALIZATION DEFINED

As a child grows, he develops in many ways. Physically he becomes taller, heavier, stronger, and capable of such activities as walking, talking, writing, riding a bicycle, and, later, having sex relations. Mentally he becomes capable of such activities as memorizing poems, working out problems in algebra, imagining love scenes, and learning the knowledge necessary to carry through a job. He also develops a more or less consistent personality structure so that he can be characterized, for example, as shy, modest, bold, persistent, frugal, or friendly. However, such lines of development in themselves are of limited value in explaining how someone functions in the society. They do not tell us, for example, what behavior to expect from a doctor or a department store clerk, what hardware stores or hospitals are for, what utensils to use when eating specific foods, how to behave in church, or what to do if giving a party. Nor do they touch on the feelings an individual develops towards his sister, his pastor, his fraternity, his country. Nor do they indicate the standards of right and wrong he upholds or his feelings if he is inadvertently rude, fails an examination, or, in some other way, does not measure up to his own expectations or the expectations of others.

The baby of course knowns nothing of these ways of his society; but he has the potentialities to learn them.

His potentialities in fact are wide and varied. In one set-ting he will speak English, in another, Russian; in one he will eat rice with chopsticks, in another, with a fork; in one he will stand and feel proud if "La Marseillaise" is played, in another the music would have to be "God Save the Queen"; in one he will be deeply respectful to his father, in another he will speak to him as a "pal"; in one he will feel somber and serious at a funeral, in another he will feel and express strong emotion; in one he will eat grasshoppers with relish, in another he will turn away in disgust.

It is with such questions that the socialization of the child is concerned. We may define socialization as *the process by which someone learns the ways of a given society or social group so that he can function within it.* Socialization includes both the learning and internalizing of appropriate patterns, values, and feelings. The child ideally not only knows what is expected of him and be-haves accordingly; he also feels that this is the proper way for him to think and behave. The term *socialization,* in itself, refers to learning the ways of any established and continuing group—an immigrant becomes socialized into the life of his new country; a recruit into the life of the Army; a new insurance agent into the patterns of his com-pany and his job. Socialization of the child has a broader application—the child ultimately becomes an adult human being who has learned the ways of the ongoing society. The meaning of socialization can be clarified by citing some problems which are not directly relevant to the socialization process.

First, it is not a problem of socialization to explain, or speculate upon, how a society or social group began. The society into which the child is born, with its common expectations, ways of doing things, standards of right and wrong, and current trends, is the result of a unique his-torical evolution and exists before the child enters it. Socialization begins with the assumption of this ongoing pre-existing society.

Second, socialization is not concerned with the impact

of new members on the society or on given groups. Socialization is not strictly a one-way process. The entrance of a new member into a family, or into any unit, changes the group. It is not just the old group with one added person; it is a *new* group with new relationships and a new organization. But only insofar as the interrelationships affect the socialization process is this new reorganization directly relevant to our interests.

Third, it is not a problem of socialization to explain the uniqueness of individuals. Although it is true that no two individuals are alike and that each person has a singular heredity, distinctive experiences, and a unique personality development, socialization focuses not on such individualizing patterns and processes but on similarities, on those aspects of development which concern the learning of, and adaptation to, the culture and society.

Finally, it is not a problem of socialization to explain how the basic drives and needs of an individual are developed and elaborated. From the perspective of socialization, the child is not viewed primarily as a possessor of drives and needs which require satisfaction, but rather as someone who is capable of learning the patterns, symbols, expectations, and feelings of the surrounding world.

Since the socialization process occurs through social relationships, it is generally considered to be a subject of study for the social psychologist or sociologist. A child cannot learn the ways of the society by being apart from people; others, wittingly or unwittingly, teach him through their guidance, examples, responses, and emotional attachments. Thus socialization is a function of social interaction.

This Study deals with the process of socialization, with the problem of how the child becomes a functioning member of the society. We shall use a wide range of illustrations, but generally they will come from our own North American society and from the middle-class groups with which we are most familiar. In Chapter 2 we shall discuss the basic preconditions for socialization, to be followed by a consideration in Chapter 3 of the mechanisms and tech-

niques by which it occurs. Chapter 4 is concerned with
the primary socializing agencies in our society—the family, school, peer group, and media of mass communication.
Socialization is intimately related to family life, and, although the family is treated as such only in Chapter 4,
ramifications of this relationship are discussed at various
points in the Study. Chapter 5 considers socialization patterns of certain basic subdivisions in our society—social
class, ethnic group, and community, particularly "suburbia." The final chapter is a brief analysis of socialization
patterns and processes in relation to developments in later
life.

2 PRECONDITIONS FOR SOCIALIZATION

For a child to become socialized, three preconditions are necessary. First, there must be an ongoing society, the world into which he is to be socialized. Second, the child must have the requisite biological inheritance. If he is feeble-minded or suffers from a serious mental disorder, adequate socialization becomes extremely difficult, if not impossible. Third, a child requires "human nature," defined as the ability to establish emotional relationships with others and to experience such sentiments as love, sympathy, shame, envy, pity, and awe. Each of these necessary preconditions is also significant insofar as it points up basic background material for an understanding of socialization.

An Ongoing Society

A child is born into a world that already exists. From the point of view of society, the function of socialization is to transmit the culture and motivation to participate in established social relationships to new members. The society has a patterned consistency so that one can predict, within limits, how people will behave, think, and feel. We may view this society from several perspectives, each of which points up certain distinctive features.

First, there is the perspective of *norms* and *values*.

7

Norms refer to those patterns of behavior that are common in the society or a given social group and are more or less taken for granted. Thus, in our society, men wear trousers and shirts and women—although less so today—wear dresses; men shake hands when they are introduced to one another; we say "hello" when we answer the phone; we express sympathy when we meet someone who has just suffered some tragic loss. There are also values, those ideas which we hold to be right and wrong. So, for example, in some groups, it is considered worthy to contribute to charity, to be loyal to one's friends, and to express feelings of patriotism, and it is considered wrong to snub old friends, marry for money, or have an affair with someone else's wife.

A second perspective is that of *status* and *role*. A status is a position in the social structure, and a role is the expected behavior of someone who holds a given status. We can cooperate with others because we know the rights and obligations associated with each status. The taxi driver has the right to ask for your fare and the obligation to drive you to your destination; the doctor has the right to ask about your symptoms and, in some instances, to have you remove your clothes; and he has the obligation to try to cure you. Similarly, role behavior is expected of the teacher, student, mother, father, daughter, grocery clerk, Roman Catholic, taxicab passenger, and doctor's patient. Each person has many statuses which define his expected behavior in given situations.

A third perspective is that of *institutions*, each of which focuses about a segment of life and consists of many norms and statuses. One such institution is the school, whose primary function is to transmit, in a more or less formal way, a large share of the intellectual traditions of a society. Within the school there are norms relating to attendance, sports events, courses, and holiday celebrations; and patterned status relationships among the teachers, students, principal, and custodians. The church, hospital, stock market, and congressional system are other examples of institutions which are the foci for the organization of many activities. These institutions continue to operate over a period of many years despite a regular turn-over of personnel because each new generation is "social-ized" into the appropriate patterns.

A fourth perspective focuses on cultural and group subdivisions within the larger society. One major subdivi-sion is *social class*. Individuals in our society vary in the amount of wealth, prestige, and power they possess, and associated with these are differences in values and ways of life. Social class rankings may partake of all of these elements. At one extreme may be the upper-class individ-ual who is wealthy, has an important business position, lives in a luxurious home, sends his children to private schools, and vacations in Europe. At the other extreme may be the lower-class individual who works as an un-skilled laborer, left school at the age of fourteen, lives in a slum area, and has "crude" table manners. Between these extremes there are other rough rankings, from the profes-sional man and lesser business executive to the white collar worker to the skilled laborer. It is evident that no single characteristic clearly differentiates class groups, that the lines between them are blurred, and that there is con-siderable inter-class movement. But a stratification system of a kind does exist.

Another major subdivision in our society, one which overlaps considerably with social class, is the *ethnic group*. The population of North America has been built up of immigrants from many countries. In coming here they have kept some of their old-country characteristics and they may be thought of as "different," both by others and by themselves. Thus we find Italians, Greeks, Jews, Mexi-cans, Anglo-Saxons, and French Canadians who are dis-tinguished from others by their names, language, tradi-tional foods, holiday rituals, occupations, folklore, patterns of child rearing, and loyalties. A related division is the *racial minority*, which is also likely to be thought of as "different" both by others and by themselves. The most prominent racial minority in our society is the Negro.

Still another perspective is that of *social change*. The

society into which a child is born is not static; there are conflicting pressures, a diffusion of materials and ideas, and general trends. For example, one can trace over a period of time the movement of families to the suburbs; the increasing emancipation of women; changing patterns of child rearing; the development of new careers in new industries; and the tendency to professionalization of teachers, morticians, social workers, insurance agents, pharmacists, and other groups. The society in which the child lives today is very different from the society in which he will live a generation from now.

There is, then, a complex and variable world, which may be approached from many perspectives, into which the child is to be socialized. In order to function within it, he must have at least a minimum of knowledge about this world and a minimum of what the culture defines as the appropriate feelings. He must know what to expect from people of given statuses, how he himself fits in with the various groupings, what is considered proper and improper in given situations, and the range of acceptable behavior in those segments of social life which are rapidly changing. This is the world which the socializers, knowingly or unknowingly, pass on to the newcomer.[1]

Biological Inheritance

A second precondition for socialization is an adequate biological inheritance, or original nature. It is apparent that those who have certain serious hereditary deficiencies either cannot be socialized or will have distinctive problems in the process. For example, a child born with a serious brain injury may find it difficult to remember; or a child born deaf cannot, since he does not hear his own voice, learn to use language without special training. Even for the biologically normal individual, however, it is important for an understanding of socialization to consider original nature.

Our biological inheritance permits socialization. We are helpless and completely dependent at birth, but with

the ⋯ the brain, physical organs, and nervous ⋯ ome capable of complex and profound
acti— ⋯ and manipulate concepts and symbols,
ima ⋯ in the past or future, identify with the
fee_ ⋯ ghts of others, and internalize standards
an(⋯ ich we guide our behavior. In sum, our
he⋯ s to understand the ongoing society, to
fu⋯ , to judge it, and to modify it.

ti⋯ inheritance not only permits socializa-
a⋯ s it. Many newborn creatures are helpless
th⋯ at birth, but for no other creature does
b⋯ cy last so long. Lower forms of life, animals,
f⋯ sects, can often function well merely by
it⋯ ral instincts. The bird knows how to build
t⋯ beaver its dam; the bee knows what foods
li⋯ particular job it has in the colony, and the
T⋯ to hunt and how to protect its young.
u⋯ rn patterns that have persisted relatively
⋯ thousands of years. No comparable built-in
mechanisms exist in human beings, and, in order to function within society, we must learn from others how to
build homes, earn a living, and take care of our children.

In trying to understand human behavior, it is of little
use to ask what proportion derives from original nature
and what proportion from environment, for they are so
closely and inevitably intertwined. The interrelationships
of the two, insofar as they relate to socialization, can best
be seen if we consider certain inherited characteristics.
Thus we are born with potentialities for a certain body
build, tendencies to mature physically at a certain pace,
and such physical characteristics as skin color, eye color,
and hair texture. In and of themselves, these characteristics and tendencies allow us to do little more than distinguish certain individuals and groups. However, they obvi-
ously are of more than classificatory significance in our
society, for they are given social definitions and evalu-
ations. It is not the physical characteristics in themselves
of Negroes which explain why they are refused admission
to certain private clubs or denied access to certain jobs.

It is the social status of Negroes—the understanding of which requires considerable historical and social analysis —which underlies these limitations. So likewise is it basically a social definition if we consider blonde hair and a "good figure" desirable in a girl, or tallness and an athletic build desirable in a boy, or early teething and walking in a child.

Also inherited are certain needs or drives such as hunger, thirst, sleep, and sex expression, which, too, are socially defined. The need for food may be satisfied by eating meat, vegetables, insects, or even people. The sex needs may be expressed directly or "sublimated" in dancing, art, or religious ceremonies; they may be directed towards people within or without certain groups; they may be suppressed before marriage or encouraged and directed to certain specific outlets.

A child likewise inherits temperamental tendencies, towards passivity or activity, perhaps towards restlessness, temper, or certain sensitivities. Such tendencies are evidenced almost from birth in a baby's movements, sleeping and crying habits, and responses to food. These temperamental tendencies, however, cannot be divorced from the interpretations of others who react to such activities and sensitivities with annoyance, pleasure, or even lack of apparent response. These reactions affect both the subsequent demonstrations of, and feelings towards, such temperament.

Similarly, the development of intelligence and particular talents cannot be separated from the surrounding world. Whether or not the given potentiality is actually developed, and what direction it takes, depends on the possibilities that are available, the encouragement that comes from others, and the growth of the personality structure. Einstein, Mozart, and Mickey Mantle would not have become, respectively, a famous scientist, composer, and baseball player if, when they were infants, their parents had moved to an isolated Eskimo village and remained there the rest of their lives. Nor would these men have been successful if their personalities were so disturbed that they could not focus their attention long enough to develop their talents and abilities.

A child inherits in addition certain "mass movements," impulses which are expressed in random undefined directions. For example, he makes numerous different types of sounds and moves his fingers in a variety of ways. Whether these sounds are organized into the English, Spanish, or Chinese languages, or whether the finger movements include the ability to write, manipulate utensils, or play musical instruments, are functions of the specific definitions and guidance given by people in the surrounding world.

It is apparent that certain biological requisites are necessary for an adequate socialization. In actual situations, however, these biological factors become so closely interlinked with elements of the social world that it is impossible to isolate empirically the hereditary from the environmental and to weight the importance of each.

Human Nature

A third precondition for socialization is what C. H. Cooley calls "human nature." This term has been variously defined and used. But some of the definitions and usages do not clearly distinguish human life from animal life, and others suggest that human nature, rather than being universal to man, varies with the cultural setting and context. Cooley's usage does distinguish human nature from the nature of other animals and applies generally to all human beings.[2]

To Cooley, human nature is made up of the basic sentiments of man, of such feelings as love, shame, vanity, ambition, envy, hero-worship, and cruelty. Admittedly these sentiments vary and are expressed differently in different cultures, but the existence of such sentiments is universal. Having these sentiments implies the ability to empathize with others, to place oneself imaginatively in their positions and to feel as they do. The lower animals, although they have the ability to form emotional attachments, do not, as far as we know, have the capacity to empathize. We assume, for example, that a cat that toys with a mouse is unaware of the feelings of the mouse and therefore is not, in Cooley's sense, "cruel," nor is a large dog that attacks a small one and takes his bone "unkind." However, a prison guard who tortures a prisoner or refuses him food is very much aware of the prisoner's suffering. That human nature, as so defined, is universal among human beings is suggested by the fact that we can come to understand the feelings and behavior of people whose way of life is different from our own. Travelers, anthropologists, missionaries, and soldiers often find it difficult at first to understand the feelings of native groups, but sooner or later they can establish personal relationships and feel rapport with them.

This human nature, Cooley suggests, is not part of our original inheritance; it develops in primary groups—the family, or a child's playmates—in which relationships are face to face and in which feelings are close, intimate, and intense.[3] And practically all human beings have human nature, since practically all, no matter where they live, are brought up in primary group settings.

Such a conception of human nature is not a scientifically precise one, and some of the specific case materials that may be cited to support it are open to question. However, there is a mass and variety of evidence which points to some sentimental and emotional core to human life, and this core, this human nature, becomes a precondition for socialization; without it, proper social development does not occur. Evidence for this comes from varied sources.

Isolated Children. Numerous reports have been published of children reared in modern society, but in relative isolation. The best-authenticated cases are those of Anna and Isabelle.[4] Anna was an illegitimate child, confined to one room from infancy. She had very little contact with other human beings. The mother brought her milk but otherwise paid little attention to her, not ordinarily taking the trouble to bathe, train, supervise, or cuddle her. When Anna was found, at the age of six, she showed few, if any, signs of human nature. She was described as completely apathetic; she lay on her back, immobile, expressionless, and indifferent. She was believed to be deaf and possibly blind. She lived for another five years, first in a country home and later in a foster home and school for retarded children, and in this period developed only to the level of the normal two-year-old. Whether the lack of development was due primarily to mental deficiency, to the deprivations of early life, or a combination of the two, is not clear.

Isabelle's circumstances were relatively more fortunate. She too was an illegitimate child, kept in seclusion. However, her deaf-mute mother was shut off with her and the two were able to communicate by gestures. When Isabelle was found, also at the age of six, she too lacked a manifest human nature. She seemed utterly unaware of ordinary social relationships and reacted to strangers almost like an animal, with fear and hostility. She made only a strange croaking sound and in many respects her actions resembled those of deaf children. In contrast to Anna, Isabelle was given a systematic and skillful program of training and, after a very slow beginning, began to develop quite rapidly. By the time she was eight and a half years old, she had reached a normal educational level and was described as bright, cheerful, and energetic. Thus, with an appropriate environment, she was able to develop into a girl with normal habits and feelings. It is to be noted, however, that Isabelle, in contrast to Anna, most certainly had an adequate intelligence potential and did have close, although limited, human contact when she was a baby.

"Deprivation" and Psychopaths. A second type of evidence comes from psychiatry. Many instances have been reported of children who, though not isolated from society, received as infants little attention and affection and did not establish any strong interpersonal ties or primary relationships with other human beings. Psychiatrists speak of them as suffering "deprivation." In some cases these

children had a succession of ministering adults; in others
they were in institutions in which there were few adults
to look after them. René Spitz reports on one such case
in an institution in which there were 91 children, none
older than three.[5] To take care of 45 infants less than
eighteen months old, there were only six nurses. For most
of the day, these infants lay on their backs in small
cubicles, without human contact. Within the first year, the
average score of all the children on developmental tests fell
from 124 to 72. Two years later a follow-up study found
that over one-third of the 91 children had died and the 21
who were still at the institution were extraordinarily retarded. Despite the fact that conditions became much more
favorable for children when they reached fifteen months,
with more nurses and more opportunities for joint play
activity, their heights and weights were below average,
many could not walk or use a spoon, only one could dress
himself, and only two had a vocabulary of more than five
words. Spitz concludes that the conditions of the first year
were so detrimental both physically and psychologically
that the subsequent more favorable conditions could not
counteract the damage.

Another case reported from India tells of a so-called
feral child, a child who had been separated from society
when still a baby and allegedly reared by wolves.[6] The
child, then about eight years old and called Kamala, was
discovered in a cave in 1921 by a British missionary and
lived for over eight years in the missionary school. When
found, Kamala had few "human" characteristics. She wore
no clothing, ate raw meat, lowered her mouth to her food,
had impassive facial features, and showed only hostility
to human beings. During her stay at the school, Kamala
never reached a normal level for her age, but she did
make considerable progress, especially after she developed
an emotional attachment to the missionary's wife. She
learned to eat cooked food, wear a dress, understand simple language, to like other children, and to express various
kinds of emotion. An analysis by Bruno Bettelheim
strongly suggests that the wolf-rearing part of the story is

a myth,[7] but without doubt Kamala had suffered extreme emotional isolation. To use Cooley's terms, Kamala had no human nature when she was found; she was developing it in the close personal contacts of the missionary school.

Psychiatrists suggest that lack of early primary relations is also responsible for many psychopathic personalities.[8] The psychopath is someone who is almost completely self-centered. His relations with others are superficial; he is quite incapable of caring for others or of establishing emotional ties with them. He seems to have no internalized standards of right and wrong, no feelings of guilt, and often shows a general lack of concern in situations which ordinarily arouse some emotional response. When this type of person becomes delinquent, rehabilitation is extremely difficult. According to Cooley, such psychopaths have never developed a real human nature because they have never experienced adequate primary-group relationships.

In the ordinary course of events, the preconditions for socialization are taken for granted; only in exceptional circumstances do they come to our attention. The preconditions, in themselves, tell nothing of the process by which socialization occurs. The latter process is our central concern.

3 THE PROCESS OF SOCIALIZATION

In discussing the socialization of the child, we are not concerned with a specific culture. There are many differences in values and behavior between societies, and between subgroups within societies, but we assume that the basic elements of the process are essentially the same for peoples everywhere.

Many theories have been propounded to explain the process by which socialization occurs. Some of these theories have been derived from the observation of normal children in our society, others have their roots in the study of the emotionally disturbed, others in laboratory studies of children and animals, and still others in the study of "primitive" tribes. With such different sources of information, differences in ideas, perspectives, and interpretations are not surprising.

A further complexity is the popular interest in the subject. The general public, sometimes with traditional answers and sometimes with questions about practical problems, necessarily influences the research interests and public pronouncements of the specialists. The problems, however, are not simple, and both the application of traditional ideas and the replies of the experts have varied almost from decade to decade and from one group of specialists to another. Thus in discussing socialization we must recognize that no one theory has received general acceptance, that a certain amount of speculation is necessary, and that there is no certainty or completeness in the theories and ideas presented.

In this chapter we shall emphasize primarily a social role theory of socialization. We are not using "theory" in the sense of a logically interrelated body of propositions; rather we are referring to a particular type of conceptual orientation, one which leads us to look in certain directions. Above all else, this social role approach recognizes that a child is born into an ongoing society with common symbols, established patterns, and recognized positions, and that it is through others that a child learns these elements of the social world. Employing this general perspective, we shall discuss the stages of socialization, the behavior of "significant others," and the process of learning. We shall then contrast two different approaches to socialization: learning theory, developed by academic psychologists, and psychoanalysis, primarily developed by clinical therapists.

Social Role Theory

The key concepts in role theory are status and role. A *status* is simply a position in a social structure, and each person has many statuses—an age status, sex status, religious status, nationality status, and so on. Attached to each status is a pattern of expected behavior, a *role*. Role implies not only a knowledge of the expected behavior but also culturally appropriate values and feelings. The good soldier not only obeys his superior on the battlefield, he feels that it is right and proper for the officer to issue the commands. Roles may be general, such as sex or age, and affect behavior within a wide range of situations, or they may be as specific as catcher on a baseball team.

In order that individuals may cooperate with others, they must first have common symbols—concepts, gestures, and objects that have closely similar meanings for all. But this is not enough. They must also know the statuses and roles of others and of themselves. Complementary-type relationships show this most clearly—teacher and student, barber and customer, troop leader and Boy Scout, dentist and patient. Each knows how to behave and what to expect from the other. We ordinarily have a rich and varied repertoire of roles and can pass rapidly from one to another.

Two qualifications to this discussion of role relationships are necessary. First, we often do not find "role consensus." [1] The expectations of behavior for a particular status, especially in a society as complex as our own, may be ambiguous or may vary greatly from one person to another. The teacher, student, and parent, for example, may have quite different ideas of how the teacher should behave in the classroom. Second, an individual does not always play his role in the same way. A doctor does not act the same with each of his patients nor a father with each of his sons. And when such factors as immediate mood and social context are considered, the variations range even further. The degree of role consensus and diversities of role application are often in themselves significant problems for research and always, depending on the breadth of the particular problem, deserve greater or lesser consideration.

The role concept also serves as a bridge between the person and society. Role is related to the individual in that ideally he knows what is expected of him in a given position and has internalized appropriate attitudes and motivations. It is related to the society in that the particular expectations "pre-exist." Thus a hospital may be analyzed in terms of the duties and privileges of doctors, nurses, dietitians, patients, physiotherapists, administrators, and other status personnel without reference to any particular individual. [2]

The problem of socialization for role theory is to explain how a child comes to function within a system of statuses. How does he learn to recognize status positions, to know and internalize their expectations and accompanying values, and to act those roles that are appropriate for him? A theory of socialization is not an all-encompassing theory of human behavior. Role theory, as used here, seeks to explain in broad terms the process by which the child becomes a functioning member of the group; it does not seek to account for the unique expression in interpersonal relationships of particular opinions, attitudes, sentiments, or traits. Each person, with his distinctive heredity and experiences, comes to play his roles in a unique way. The particular integration of these role relationships for any individual is a problem not of socialization but of personality development and, as such, is a task primarily for the psychologist.[3] To focus on the individual implies a psychological point of view; to focus on the group or social relationships implies a sociological orientation. Each discipline is concerned with a different aspect of the same reality situation.

Stages of Socialization

As the child becomes socialized, the organization of his behavior becomes increasingly complex. He must integrate changes in physical growth, knowledge, status relationships, and emotional development. Although socialization is a continuous process for the child, it is sometimes convenient to think of it as involving a series of successive stages. A temporary equilibrium or level of development is reached, then new elements are introduced which lead to readjustments and new equilibria. With such a view, new developments and problems in integration stand out more clearly.

Maturation. Underlying the social development of the child is biological maturation. The biological organism, assuming a suitable environment, follows a systematic and orderly pattern in the development of neural, muscular, and glandular tissues. No amount of training can enable a person to function in given ways before he is biologically ready.

Maturation is closely related to socialization. We have previously noted that the timing and adequacy of such motor skills as manipulating a spoon or riding a bicycle, which depend on maturation, are socially judged and defined. Language, too, depends on maturation, for the appropriate nerves and muscles must be adequately developed before the child can comprehend abstract concepts or express certain sounds and link them into words and sentences. Maturation is also of basic significance in direct social relationships. The child must reach a certain development before he can distinguish one person from another, inhibit the expression of his immediate feelings, or play cooperatively with others. Still further maturation is necessary before the child can understand what another is thinking or feeling or take the position of someone else in his imagination.

The relevance of maturation to socialization is seen in the work of the Swiss psychologist, Jean Piaget, who studied nursery school children through painstaking observation, questioning, and simple experiments. Although maturation as such was not his concern, he does show that there are distinct lines of development and that quite early in a child's life social factors combine with physiological development to permeate his ways of thought and perception of the world. Underlying Piaget's research is the assumption that the child's mind is not an immature form of the adult mind; rather, the child thinks in a world of his own, a world inherently and distinctly different from that of the adult.

Piaget reports that the child, in perceiving the world or in learning elements of the culture, goes through a series of stages. In language development, the child's early speech is "egocentric"—he speaks solely to express his own nature and is incapable of considering another's point of view. As the child matures and he is able to take the position of others, he adjusts his speech to their needs or interests and his speech becomes "socialized." [4]

Similarly, a child, until he adequately matures, is unable to realize that moral judgments of behavior need not be absolute.[5] At first the young child views right as the will of the adult, later he judges behavior in terms of its consequences, and only still later is he capable of placing himself in the position of others and judging by their motives or intentions. Thus in discussing a hypothetical story, a young child may say that a boy who steals is bad; later, that a boy who is caught stealing is bad, and, at an older age, that a rich boy who steals is worse than a poor boy who steals.

Age Status and the Development of Independence. A child passes through a sequence of age statuses. As a newborn baby he has a status in the group. Certain behavior is expected of him and others modify their behavior accordingly. The child is expected to cry when he is uncomfortable, to sleep when he is sleepy, and to excrete without restraint. He is unfamiliar with the ways of the society and depends on others for care and for decisions concerning his welfare.

As his experience and capabilities increase and as he becomes familiar with his statuses, his rights and obligations change. Others come to view and treat him differently. It is expected that he will gradually become less dependent on others and will himself handle more tasks and problem situations. He will learn the language, distinguish between the behavior of boys and girls, and attend school; he will himself decide what foods to eat, how to spend his money, and what girls to take out. He will progressively have the status of the child who walks, talks, goes to school, goes out on dates, and works, each status implying greater independence. Eventually he will internalize most if not all of the ways of the society and care for and help to socialize a subsequent generation.

The distinctions of age status may be drawn finely or, as in our own society, they may be approximate. Expectations also vary in different societies and in subgroups within a society. The expectations for the Eskimo boy are different from those for the English boy, and the expectations for the farm boy vary considerably from those for the boy in the large city. Age statuses are likewise varyingly symbolized. Among some groups, there are *rites de passage*. Among many Jews, a boy of thirteen undergoes a Bar Mitzvah ceremony and only then can he take part in certain religious ceremonies. In our society, many age status symbols are associated with sex status and school year promotions. Margaret Mead cites the example in one school of an eighth-grade graduation ritual. Boys and girls begin the evening wearing blue jeans; then they separate; and when they return for the evening dance, the girls are wearing party dresses and the boys "party" suits.[6] Distinctions of this kind may be symbolized in the carrying of a house key, putting on lipstick or high-heeled shoes, and driving a car. Such symbols point up the changing age statuses of a particular child and distinguish him from his previous statuses and from those who are at lower levels.

A child learns the expectations of his age status primarily from the behavior of other people who distinguish between the expectations of the present and those of the past and future. Such phrases as "you're a big boy now," "you're too old to cry," "you can have a watch when you graduate," and "what do you want to be when you grow up?"—whether they are directed to the child in question or to someone else in his presence—suggest that a child is presumed to know the expectations and to act accordingly. Likewise, he may have tasks which correspond to these age statuses—making his own bed, walking the dog, washing the car. The child is neither to regress nor to attempt behavior "beyond his years." The child of five in many social circles is too old to be taken into his mother's bed, but too young to play with knives and matches. "Growing up" means learning new roles and relinquishing or adapting the old.

The progression through series of age statuses may be one of relative continuity or relative discontinuity. Ruth Benedict points out certain discontinuous elements in our society in socializing the son to be a prospective father.[7] As a child, a son does not have serious responsibilities; he submits to his father; and he inhibits sexual expression. In contrast, as a father, he has important adult responsibilities; he expresses authority; and he has a primary sexual role in the family—none of which he is trained for. These, she suggests, may become the foci of personal problems.

The complexities of a continuity-discontinuity perspective are many. To what degree can we anticipate discontinuity and imaginatively prepare for it? To what degree can we prepare a child to be flexible, since we know certain patterns change drastically from one generation to another? To what degree can a child substitute role behavior or sentiments? Playing at being a heroic, girl-rescuing space pilot probably does not prepare a boy for an adult occupation, but may possibly help him to assume a masculine role in relation to women.

Behavior of Significant Others

The child learns the ways of the group not through meeting the culture in the abstract, but through other people; it is they who know and carry the patterns of the society to him. Not all other people have an equal influence on the child. Some, by virtue of their particular positions or by their appearance at certain times in his life, become objects of emotional involvement and are especially significant in his development. These are his "significant others."

Significant others usually act in terms of their particular image of the child. Since this image is derived in part from general conceptions in the society, it changes as these conceptions change. In recent years, for example, through the spread of psychoanalytic ideas, middle-class groups have come to emphasize the long-run influence of early childhood training patterns. Many parents blame themselves if their children turn out badly. No longer is it acceptable, as it was a few generations ago, to speak sadly of the child born to be a "black sheep."

The image towards which others act is also derived in part from the child's particular statuses. This is clearly evident in the child of royalty; however, all children have such statuses as race, nationality, sex, social class, place of residence, and membership and birth order in a given family, which influence how others behave towards them.

Patterning of Behavior. To the child, the behavior of others is likely to have a certain consistency, organization, and predictability. The patterning of social behavior derives in part from the larger culture, for individuals ordinarily carry out the expected behavior of their statuses, and in part from the necessities of interaction, for, when individuals are together for a considerable period of time, a division of labor occurs. Thus Robert F. Bales and P. E. Slater write:

> One important aspect of the social organization of groups which endure over any considerable time is the fact that usually roles within the organization are differentiated from each other . . . overt acts of certain qualities are expected of certain persons at certain times, while overt acts of other qualities are expected of other persons at other times.[8]

Perhaps one person introduces new ideas, another smooths over disagreements, another does the necessary routine tasks.

The patterning of behavior is evident to the child in various ways—in such time and space routines as mealtimes, school preparations, and bedtime rituals; in the annual celebrations of birthdays, anniversaries, and holidays; in the interests of the mother who is regularly concerned with shopping and in maintaining contact with relatives; in the free and easy discussion of some subjects and the avoidance of others. Personality characteristics expressed in social interaction are also likely to be consistent, be they evidenced in politeness to strangers, sympathy to the sick, or self-effacement before authority figures.

Definitions of Others. Significant others define the world for the child and serve as models for his attitudes and behavior. They teach the child, in a broad sense, through bestowing rewards and inflicting punishments. These rewards are conditional. If the child behaves as the significant others desire, they give him attention, affection, gifts, or invitations to participate; if he behaves otherwise, they refuse attention, reprimand, express disappointment, withdraw expected gains, or physically punish.[9] The rewards and punishments that significant others administer need not be directly congruent with the pleasure and displeasure that the child experiences. A child may defy his father and be whipped, but the gratification he gets from his father's attention, or perhaps from annoying his father, may more than compensate for the physical pain.

Significant others teach some role behavior through direct instruction. With conscious forethought they may instruct the child in the appropriate behavior of the tennis player or, in certain parts of the United States, in the expected behavior of the white to the Negro. They may teach roles in reply to the child's questions. A child wonders what a bacteriologist does and the teacher refers to his laboratory work and the respect which the child should accord him; or a child asks about a proposed family reunion and the parents define the appropriate obligations to relatives. Gift-giving, too, may involve a more or less explicit definition of status expectations; the boy receives a model rocket ship and the girl a nursing set, or the Catholic girl a rosary and the Jewish girl a Star of David brooch.[10]

Sometimes significant others stress norms and values rather than roles. A child is told to be considerate to his dog, be polite to adults, and stick to the rules of the game. Although, for purposes of analysis, values and roles may be distinguished, in such day-to-day instances they are inseparably interlinked. Consideration for a dog is associated with the status of human being and possibly pet owner, politeness to adults with the age status of the child, and playing fairly with the status of responsible playmate.

Ordinarily, in everyday relationships, significant others refer neither to roles or values, but to the immediate situation. A child splashes water and his mother shouts at him to stop; a girl kisses her little brother and her parents beam their approval; a girl pupil flirts in the corridors and a teacher tells her to move on; a mother rehearses her child to greet an expected visitor. These references to specific situations also become organized into roles and corresponding values. The primary mechanism for this is language. Comments about St. Patrick's Day, remarks about a given church, names beginning with "Mc," jokes about Pat and Mike, and the like may all be linked together by the status concept "Irish." "Santa Claus" may link references to North Pole, reindeer, Christmas, gift-giving, charity, and a festive spirit. "Dirty boy" may refer to a child's unwashed face, soiled clothing, indecent stories, or many other types of unacceptable behavior. Writers on semantics have especially stressed the relationship between language and expected attitudes. The term "rate-buster" in a factory work group designates both the employee who produces more than others and the attitude of other workers towards him. Such school peer group terms as "big wheel," "spoke," "brain," "drip," "dope," and "mouse" serve to organize many types of opinion and specific actions.

Significant Others as Models. Significant others teach the child through their behavior in his presence and the feelings and attitudes they express. They give meaning to objects through their use of them.[11] Through using ball point pens, they define these as objects for writing; through looking at wrist watches, they indicate that they are objects for telling time, and perhaps objects for display as well. Significant others in their behavior similarly reflect values. Through reading books, they may suggest that books are important; through housework, they suggest that the home should be tidy, and possibly, through the way the work is done, that it is also a chore.

Through their interactions, significant others indicate attitudes, feelings, and expected relationships. They show the rights and obligations expected of the janitor, doctor, airline hostess, and truck driver, and, perhaps, the amount of respect which these positions merit. Through welcoming guests, they suggest the propriety of hospitality and possibly, at the same time, through fluttering about before the guests arrive and relaxing after they have gone, they also indicate the accompanying tension.[12]

Although significant others are always important in socialization, the possible variations and combinations of their behavior are almost limitless. They may be few or many; they may express a wide or narrow range of affect; they may behave with varying mixtures of confidence, hesitancy, and annoyance; they may be consistent or inconsistent; they may or may not agree with each other in the demands they make on the child; they may express any number of authority patterns. At one extreme, the models may serve as sources of simple imitation; at the other, they may establish strong emotional ties with the child and become prototypes of relatively permanent psychological characteristics.

The behavior of significant others is also closely related to the development of the child's personality structure. The same behavior on the part of significant others teaches the child the ways of the society and helps determine his personality. Whether a given child is aggressive or submissive, rigid or flexible in his thinking, whether he views outsiders as friendly or unfriendly, whether he views new situations with assurance or trepidation, his particular self-protective defenses, his ability to love—all, in part, are results of the previous behavior of significant others. His own personality make-up also strongly influences the interaction process itself. The child is an interpretive agent, never merely a passive recipient of the influences that impinge on him, and the specific impact of any particular interaction is always a function of what the child has already become and the expectations and relationships he has already formed. A graphic illustration is found in the report by Anna Freud and Sophie Dann of six Jewish refugee children whose parents had been killed in Nazi concentration camps. The children, all aged three, had been transferred as a group from camp to camp before arriving at a country house in England. They felt intense solidarity with each other and viewed all adults with suspicion and hostility. The authors write:

> During the first days after arrival they destroyed all the toys and much of the furniture. Toward the staff they behaved either with cold indifference or with active hostility. . . . At times they ignored the adults so completely that they would not look up when one of them entered the room. They would turn to an adult when in some immediate need, but treat the same person as nonexistent once more when the need was fulfilled. In anger, they would hit the adults, bite or spit. Above all, they would shout, scream, and use bad language.[13]

As we might expect, weeks of patient and sympathetic care were necessary before the children developed any significant emotional ties with adults and began to learn more acceptable patterns of behavior.

Learning Socialized Behavior

By what process does the child learn appropriate behavior and internalize status expectations? We have already observed that he must be adequately mature physically and that socialized behavior generally tends to be learned unwittingly and incidentally in interaction with other people. As the child develops, his world expands in various directions. He is capable of more physical activities, his range of knowledge increases, he becomes familiar with more objects, he comes into contact with a greater variety of people and ideas, and he becomes capable of a wider and more subtle range of feelings and expression. He also becomes increasingly aware of statuses and roles, and accordingly reorganizes his ideas, images, feelings, and conduct.

Emotional Attachments in Socialization. Learning social behavior is not just a cognitive process; it is closely associated with attachments to others. We have observed that emotional ties are necessary for the development of human nature, since a child must experience primary relationships in order to empathize with other persons and to develop a basic psychological security. Emotional attachments also underlie the motivation to learn. Because a child seeks approval and love from significant others, he is motivated to think and behave as they wish and to model his behavior after theirs. Thus he may suppress his immediate impulses and learn table manners if his mother so desires (and insists), or he may seek to do well in school if he thereby gains the good will of his parents and teachers. Later some of the patterns become habits and others, such as success striving, become part of an internalized value system. Significant others, then, if they are themselves socialized, knowingly or unknowingly teach the ways of the society and become socializing agents.

The child's expanding world comes to include more and more people and an increasing number of groups with which he identifies and feels solidarity. The first person in the child's world is his mother or some other maternal figure. First dependent on her for care, he becomes attached to her in her own right. Following the child-mother small group come those of child and father, sibling unit, and family; then friends, teachers, and possibly popular heroes and even imaginary figures; then such larger groups as the neighborhood, school, religion, and nation. Each of these "we groups" implies a "non-we group" from which it is distinguished. The early ties may not be dropped but, as they are succeeded and reintegrated with other aspects of development, they become less encompassing.

One important device for establishing group identity and solidarity is gesture and language.[14] A family or peer group has its nicknames, a school its songs and slogans, an army unit its own colorful expressions, and a nation its emotionally toned symbols. The linguist Edward Sapir writes:

> Within the confines of a particular family, for instance, the name "Georgy," having once been mispronounced "Doody" in childhood, may take on the latter form forever after; and this unofficial pronunciation . . . becomes a very im-

portant symbol indeed of the solidarity of a particular family and of the continuance of the sentiment that keeps its members together. A stranger cannot lightly take on the privilege of saying "Doody". . . . Again, no one is entitled to say "trig" or "math" who has not gone through such familiar and painful experiences as a high school or undergraduate student. The use of such words at once declares the speaker a member of an unorganized but psychologically real group. . . . "He talks like us" is equivalent to saying "He is one of us." [15]

The numerous and complex relationships between these identifications constitute in themselves a large field of study—largely encompassed currently under the heading "reference group theory" [16]—which, although not reported on here, is directly related to problems of socialization.

Role Behavior and the Self. We have seen that a child becomes familiar with numerous statuses and roles, some of which are beyond his immediate or even prospective interpersonal network, merely through seeing and hearing what goes on about him and through reading. When such observation becomes a basis for imitation, interaction, and especially self-reference, it assumes even greater significance.

Self is a key concept in explaining the development of role behavior. *Self* is sometimes used to mean the organization of personality qualities or the experience of identity. However, it is more useful in role theory in the more limited usage of George H. Mead, who, by *self,* means simply that a person is the object of his own activity; he can act towards himself as he acts towards others.[17] This is the meaning of *self* in such phrases as "talking to oneself," "proud of oneself," or "ashamed of oneself." This usage implies that a person is both subject and object; he takes a position from the outside and views his own thoughts, feelings, and actions.

The self, in this sense, is basic to role theory. The child, if he is to function in the society, must know what behavior is expected of him in such statuses as passenger,

guest, movie-goer, boyfriend, patient, cousin, and Baptist.
He must be able, through language and self-conversation,
to designate to himself that he is or is not acting appropriately. He may imaginatively rehearse possible lines of
future action. Only by seeing himself as an object can he
know how to check, guide, and judge his own behavior
and act according to others' expectations.

The infant has neither language nor a self. He cannot
take the position of others and view himself as an object;
he cannot judge his past, present, and prospective behavior. An adult, however, does have these abilities. We may
therefore ask, how does this awareness come about; how
does the self develop?

George Mead presents a theory, the framework of
which is used in the following discussion, according to
which the self develops in three continuous stages: preparatory, play, and game.[18] In the preparatory stage, a
child does not have the ability to view his own behavior.
He imitates specific actions: perhaps he bangs on the table,
claps hands, or puts a telephone receiver to his ear. In
such instances, gratification by others is likely to be the
strategic factor in learning. Others pay no attention to
"meaningless" sounds of the child, but "mama" and
"dada" bring him attention and pleased reactions, and the
child is thereby motivated to repeat and learn them. In
this case, the child is beginning to put himself in the
position of others and is developing a rudimentary self.

In the second stage, a child actually plays at specific
roles: he links together the specific behaviors which are
identified with a given status and its expectations. So a
girl does not just stroke a doll as she might stroke any soft
object, she plays at being mother and puts the doll to bed
or reprimands it for crying. Or a boy plays gunman and
threatens to shoot anyone who obstructs him. In such play,
a child takes on the role behavior of others and acts as
though he were in their position; he is beginning to act
towards himself. The girl imaginatively asks, "What is
expected of me as mother?" and the boy, "What is expected of me as gunman?" Sometimes the child, seeing

himself from the position of others, speaks of himself in the third person, as Bobby or Billy. In such play, he not only learns the behavior of the given status, but also presumably experiences how it feels to play given roles. Thus when the girl spanks her doll, she experiences a feeling of punishing; if she serves tea, she enters into the spirit of the hostess.

Talcott Parsons suggests that the patterns of our culture encourage play which befits prospective adult roles as well as avoids disturbing potentially dangerous situations.[19] Thus the girl is encouraged to play the role of mother, but not of wife; to play the latter could encourage a potentially dangerous competition for the father's love and complicate her development and family relationships.

Cooley, whose views antedate Mead's, likewise stresses the reaction of others in discussing the "looking-glass self." [20] A child behaves in a given way and others respond; the child, on the basis of the response, is pleased or displeased with what he has done. A child tells a story; whether he is pleased or embarrassed depends primarily not on his story, but on the response which his story arouses in others. He views himself from the "looking-glass" of other people.

The "looking-glass self" not only helps us to understand a child's immediate behavior but has long-run personality implications as well. A child plays practical jokes on guests, and significant others laugh at his performance and call him "clever." The child is pleased with himself and seeks to be a "clever boy" again, and soon the "clever boy" role, temporarily or permanently, may become part of his personality structure. Consciously or not, some roles are encouraged, others discouraged.

In the play stage, according to Mead, a child forms many objects of himself and passes from one role to another in an unorganized and inconsistent manner. He has no unified conception of himself and no unitary standpoint from which he views his own behavior.

The game stage involves a further development. The child finds himself in situations in which he must respond to the expectations of several people at the same time. In playing baseball or football, the child must be aware of the possible actions of each of the players. Out of the concrete roles of particular persons, the child abstracts a composite role for himself. The child, in effect, asks what is expected of him and of others from the generalized standpoint of the team and the game. The same principle applies to any rituals or common tasks which involve collaboration or a division of assignments. Thus, on the basis of his group relationships and expectations, he comes to view himself from the position of the group, from what Mead calls the *generalized other*.

As the child develops, the generalized other becomes an internalized model consisting of the standards from which he views and judges his own behavior, the perspective which determines whether he is pleased or displeased with himself. It includes also the set of expectations for his own behavior and for others, expectations which are necessarily situations of interaction. The role of schoolboy, for example, implies both the actions of his teacher and schoolmates to him, and his actions to them; the role of the bus passenger includes the expected responses of the bus driver and the other passengers. A reciprocal interaction framework is learned and internalized.

The concept of generalized other further implies that a given individual may be consistent in his behavior and thoughts even though he moves in varying social environments. The English colonial official in Africa who drank afternoon tea and dressed for dinner is a classic example. The salesman who considers good will to be all-important, no matter which group he happens to be with, is another. Each has internalized a more or less permanent set of standards and expectations from which he views and judges the world.

In sum, the child learns roles and socialized behavior through a combination of techniques, but the direction of development depends basically on the reactions of others and the development of a self.

Two Other Theories of Socialization

Other students of human behavior have different theoretical orientations towards socialization. Two prominent and widely accepted views are *psychoanalysis* and *psychological learning theory*. Within both, there are specific theories and logically interrelated propositions; however, both, like our "role theory," are also approaches or conceptual orientations. They introduce ideas and concepts that direct the observer to select certain aspects of development for focus and emphasis.

Although the orientations of these three approaches lead to selection of different problems, they should not be thought of as alternative theories; to a considerable extent, they are complementary and not inconsistent. Some ideas of psychoanalysis and learning theory, it will be evident, have in fact been incorporated into our discussion of role theory.

In general, psychoanalysis and learning theory are less socially oriented than role theory; but both also assume that a child ordinarily learns socialized behavior incidentally and unwittingly in the course of interaction, and that social patterns are not likely to be learned and reinforced unless, in some way or another, they are gratifying. Of necessity, psychoanalytic and learning theory are presented here in limited and simplified forms. Both are complex and, within each, the disagreements among the specialists are sharp and varied.

Psychoanalysis. Although psychoanalysis is a technique of therapy and method of research as well as a theory of human behavior, we shall restrict our discussion to the latter, and then only insofar as the theory relates to socialization. Generally, "psychoanalysis," in its more limited usage, refers only to those theories developed by Sigmund Freud and carried on by his direct followers; in its wider usage, it includes a multitude of ideas which have been derived from the work of Freud and variously elaborated by other analysts and researchers. Ours is the first usage.[21]

The theory of psychoanalysis, in contrast to role theory, has been derived primarily from clinical studies of emotionally disturbed individuals. It assumes, however, that the mechanisms of behavior are similar for all human beings and that the differences between the normal and abnormal are differences in degree.

Freud postulates a distinctive type of mental structure. The child is born with an *id*, a complex of instinctual erotic drives which guides activity in keeping with the "pleasure principle." The infant does not naturally want to grow up; he is interested solely in obtaining comfort and gratification for himself. As he develops, he is restrained in various ways by his parents. He cannot always vent his anger; he must be weaned and toilet trained; he cannot play with every object that interests him. As a consequence, a portion of the id is transformed into the *ego*, that conscious aspect of personality which seeks to bring the pleasure demands under control and guide activity in keeping with the "reality principle."

Material which the ego finds difficult to handle is ordinarily repressed and lodged in what Freud calls the "unconscious"—a powerful force that finds expression in dreams, reveries, gestures, mental illnesses, psychosomatic disturbances, and innumerable aspects of interpersonal relations.

Socialization, according to psychoanalytic theory, is probably best seen in a developmental framework. There are certain basic and inevitable, although overlapping, stages of development. The first is the *oral* phase, so-called because the child derives his first erotic gratifications from the mouth. In this phase, the child comes to differentiate between the self, in the sense of identity, and the non-self and, since he receives sucking pleasure, food, and warmth primarily from his mother, forms a strong emotional attachment to her. How the infant's oral needs are met—whether he is readily satisfied, how often he is frustrated, the suddenness of weaning—is an important determinant

of the child's subsequent personality structure and interpersonal relationships. Psychoanalyst Irene M. Josselyn
writes:

> An infancy in which a child finds nursing satisfaction will
> . . . provide a feeling of comfortable security in the world
> about him so that he sees it as a friendly place in which
> to live, rather than an indifferent or attacking environment
> against which he must protect himself.[22]

The oral is followed by the *anal* phase, so-called because the child experiences pleasure in excretion and
because toilet training becomes a central problem. He
ordinarily learns toilet training because he develops an attachment to his parents. They make demands on him,
and, if he cooperates, he gains their love and approval.
Dorothy Burlingham and Anna Freud thus explain certain problems of young children in World War II who
were evacuated from London to a residential nursery.
The children often reacted to the sudden separation from
their mothers by reverting to wetting and soiling themselves. When, however, after a few months, the children
succeeded in forming adequate new relationships with
mother-substitutes, they again became "trained." [23]

The child at this stage also develops a certain autonomy,
and, when others ask that he exert self-control, he may or
may not cooperate. Here too the particular handling of the
child has long-run repercussions. Whether his parents are
severe or lenient in their training, whether they sharply
distinguish between the clean and the dirty, how they permit him to express his aggressive feelings, how they punish him for defiance—all of these affect the child's personal and social development. To quote one psychoana-
lytically oriented psychologist:

> Fantasies may also show up in the personality far removed
> from where they started, their beginnings completely dis-
> guised. The little boy, for instance, who held in his bowel
> movements in order to annoy and punish his mother may
> become the man who holds on to his money and is stingy
> with his wife and family.[24]

In the next phase, the *phallic,* in which the child, at about the age of two or three, becomes interested in his genitals as a source of gratification, the central phenomenon is the "Oedipus complex." A child's attachment to the parent of the opposite sex becomes compounded with the competing demands of the parent of the same sex, leading to feelings of hostility to the latter. The paths of development are somewhat different for the boy and the girl. The boy becomes erotically attached to his mother, wants her exclusive love, and feels jealous of his father whom he views as a rival for the mother's affection. However, the parents do not allow the boy to gain his ends. They threaten him with punishment, symbolically with castration, and he comes to repress his erotic feelings towards his mother.

The girl, in this phase, becomes strongly attached to her father and feels hostile and jealous towards her mother. Contributing to the girl's hostility is the feeling that her mother is to blame for her lack of male sex organs. But the girl too, in the ordinary course of development, is prohibited or shamed out of her love-choice, and, fearing punishment and loss of love, represses her erotic desires towards her father.

> [All children] wonder not only about their own bodies but about the bodies of others, and are more or less concerned with similarities and differences between the sexes and between grownups and themselves. . . . To a lesser or greater degree all little girls wonder if they may perhaps have lost that appendage that seems to be most highly prized and all little boys worry for fear that they may lose theirs; all little girls make up stories about getting rid of mother and marrying father and all little boys make up stories about getting rid of father and marrying mother. These things are a normal part of growing up.[25]

Perhaps the most important psychoanalytic concepts relating to socialization are *identification* and *superego,* which are particularly important in the development of the *latency* phase. In this phase, which begins at about the age of six, the erotic desires of the child are repressed and the energy which has been devoted to them is diverted primarily into an attachment to the parent of the same sex. When the child is very young, he does as his parents wish in order to avoid being punished or to win their affection. In this phase, however, through emotional identification, he places himself in the position of his parents and introjects the standards they affirm; he now behaves as they do and wish because he believes their ideas are right.

Superego is a complementary concept. The child's personality structure, composed of id and ego, now, through identification, also develops a superego. The superego, quoting Freud, is an agency which:

> . . . continues to carry on the functions which have hitherto been performed by the corresponding people in the external world; it observes the ego, gives it orders, corrects it and threatens it with punishments, exactly like the parents whose place it has taken. We . . . are aware of it, in its judicial functions, as our conscience.[26]

The superego becomes particularly relevant to socialization when the standards that are internalized accord with the patterns of the surrounding society and the groups of which the child is a member. It implies, in role theory terms, that the child has developed a self and views his own feelings and behavior from some external position. Thus, although the superego and Mead's generalized other are key ideas of quite different conceptual schemes (and different origins), they both stress the necessity of self-interaction.

In the next stage of development, the *genital* phase, which begins with puberty, the child must cope with his reawakened sexual impulses. In the normal course of development, he is no longer interested in his parents as erotic objects; he seeks satisfaction through relations with others of the opposite sex. How he handles these problems depends in part on the conditions of his immediate environment and in part on his previous development. The adolescent may be so frustrated in his immediate life that he regresses to overdependency or other infantile satisfactions, or the reinforced sexual drives may clash with standards of behavior of the superego and lead to sharp internalized conflict.

Through movies, magazine articles, lectures by child psychologists, and the like, the ideas of psychoanalysis have extended widely into the popular culture, and, especially among educated folk, have been incorporated into the patterns of child rearing. Parents now widely acknowledge the child's interest in his body and sex and the importance of nursing, weaning, toilet training, and other infant experiences. We have here the conditions for what Robert Merton calls a "self-fulfilling prophecy." [27] Certain parents accept Freud's ideas, follow his precepts in rearing their children, and in so doing find the Freudian ideas "confirmed." Alternative explanations and ways of behaving do not breach the circle.

Learning Theory. Although there are many variations of learning theory, there are certain common lines of agreement. Learning, as used by psychologists, is a broad term, applying to all behavior—motor, mental, and social— which derives from training procedures; only maturational developments are omitted. Socialization is that limited aspect of learning that concerns social behavior among human beings. The same concepts and principles that apply to lower animal forms presumably apply to human beings. Therefore it has been considered legitimate to derive basic ideas from laboratory and experimental work with rats, dogs, and other animals. Young children have also commonly been research subjects.

Learning theory researchers attempt ordinarily to break down behavior into measurable stimuli and responses and to derive the principles by which they are linked. They seek to explain how a subject learns to give old responses to new stimuli and new responses to any stimuli. The former is often explained by conditioning; the latter by "reinforcement," although the lines between the two are rather blurred. Two familiar experiments made many years ago by Pavlov, the Russian psychologist, and the

American, John B. Watson, illustrate conditioning. A dog
secretes saliva when it is shown food. Pavlov rang a bell
at the same time that food was presented to the dog. This
was repeated a number of times. Later the dog salivated
merely on hearing the sound of the bell. Watson's experiment was much less precise, but the broad principle
is similar. An infant is startled and upset when he hears a
sudden, loud, close noise. Watson showed an infant a white
rat, and, every time the infant reached for the rat, struck
a steel bar behind his head. After several repetitions the
infant was startled and upset merely at the sight of the
rat. Again the baby gave an old response to a new stimulus.[28]

Learning by reinforcement, which explains the development of new responses, introduces the concept of drive
reduction. According to the analysis of John Dollard and
Neal Miller,[29] four conditions must be considered—drives,
cues, responses, and rewards. It is assumed, first, that the
child has tension-creating drives which lead to activity.
Perhaps the child wishes parental attention, a drive; he
becomes aware of his parents playing "peek-a-boo," a
cue; he responds by also playing "peek-a-boo," and is rewarded in that he obtains attention. Or perhaps a boy has
an appetite for candy, a drive; he hears his grandfather's
footsteps, a cue; he responds by running to his grandfather, and is rewarded by eating candy which the grandfather offers. In both instances the child's particular drive
is reduced and the child, assuming he continues the activity, has learned new behavior.

This is the barest skeleton of psychological learning
theory. Many further distinctions and elaborations are
made. Thus primary drives, such as thirst and hunger, may
become the basis for secondary drives, such as approval
and attention; stimuli or cues are discriminated and generalized; responses are extinguished as well as reinforced
and may be anticipatory as well as immediate; rewards
such as food and sleep are primary, money and prestige
are learned in the culture.

In explaining socialization, a key concept is imitation.

Miller and Dollard view imitation as a response pattern which occurs under given conditions as a result of the learning process. In seeking to reduce his drives, a child imitates the behavior of others. The imitative behavior may be "matched-dependent" or "copying." In the former, the child matches another's behavior although he does not follow the other's cues. For example, a young child learns to run to greet the mailman, but only because his mother does so, not because he understands the mother's interest in mail. In copying, the child learns new behavior essentially through imitative trial and error. Perhaps through watching a skilled tennis player, and then practicing, he learns how to move into position for a backhand stroke. In both types of imitation, behavior which is rewarded is reinforced and behavior which is not is extinguished. The rewards for imitation may come from such diverse sources as physical pleasures, compliments from others, and self-approval.

Learning theory research, since it has developed largely through laboratory work, is ordinarily more precise and controlled than role theory or psychoanalysis. It is often possible, for example, to measure the extent of a drive or to regulate the strength of a stimulus. Learning theory has been most illuminating in research with animals and young children or with adults when the situations are relatively simple. It has been less successful in attempting to explain social situations involving self-judgments, ambivalent feelings, conflicting group norms, and complex motivations.

Since role theory, psychoanalysis, and learning theory have such different orientations and set different problems for themselves, they are not really alternate theories of socialization. Role theory focuses on the cognitive and emotional aspects of interaction in a patterned society, more or less taking it for granted that human beings are motivated to act and can form affective relationships. Psychoanalysis, with its clinical orientation,[30] centers on individual personality development, stressing especially the development and significance of emotional attachments. Learning theory focuses on the process by which learning, as such, takes place, independent of particular settings and statuses. Thus, to a certain degree, each theory has a different conception of what is important in socialization and each takes for granted or glosses over the central problem of others.

4 AGENCIES OF SOCIALIZATION

Socialization occurs in many settings and in interaction with many people. For purposes of analysis, it is helpful to distinguish between organized groups, such as the family, church, school, and peer group, and settings, such as the media of mass communication, that have significant characteristics in common. We speak of both groups and settings as *agencies of socialization*.

Each agency socializes the child into its own patterns and its own values. The family has certain rituals, the school its rules of order, the child peer group its codes and games, and the media of mass communication their traditional forms and story plots. Moreover, each agency —and this is more significant for our purposes—helps to socialize the child into the larger world. Parents, teachers, peers, and mass media are surrogates of wider social and cultural orders, and their impact extends beyond their own organizational limits.

Common cultural images of the child affect many agencies. Is the child basically good or bad? Are his potentialities predetermined or subject to considerable environmental influence? Does the child have specific needs that must be satisfied in particular ways or generalized needs that may be variously satisfied? Contrast the image held by Puritan early American teachers, clergymen, and parents which:

> . . . taught that natural man was wholly vile, corrupt, and prone to evil; that he could do no good without God's assistance; that he thoroughly deserved to broil in hell for eternity, and would do so if he did not grasp the hand of grace proffered him by a merciful God, through Jesus Christ.[1]

with the once extensively believed statement of John B. Watson:

> Give me a dozen healthy infants, well-formed, and my own specified world to bring them up in, and I'll guarantee to take any one at random and train him to become any type of specialist I might select—doctor, lawyer, artist, merchant-chief and, yes, even beggerman and thief, regardless of his talents, penchants, tendencies, abilities, vocations, and race of his ancestors.[2]

These views are too simple (and extreme) to be widely accepted today; current images are likely to be much more complex and to vary considerably depending on the groups under consideration.

Cultural trends also affect all agencies. If women are gaining more important statuses in the society, this may be manifested in family models, authority positions of female teachers, juvenile girl gangs, and heroines of popular movies. Or if there are increasing technical achievements, this may be manifested in household gadgets, school curricula, science or "hot rod" clubs, and television story plots.

The Family

The first and most important socializing agency is the family. In our society, the family is not as all-encompassing as it once was. Among many groups, children now attend nursery school or summer camps at the age of three and watch television when even younger. Schools, hospitals, government agencies, and service industries have

taken over many of the functions which were once considered routine for the family. Yet, for the child, the family remains the major agency of socialization. It is a
primary group whose close, intense, and enduring emotional attachments are, as we have observed, crucial not
only as the prototypes of subsequent ties, but also for
adequate socialization and emotional development of the
child. The family is the first unit with which the child has
continuous contact and the first context in which socialization patterns develop; it is a world with which he has
nothing to compare.

The Family in the Community. The family, as a socializing agent, necessarily transmits only segments of the wider
culture to the child, the particular segments depending
primarily on its social positions in the community. The
family as a unit—and it is so viewed both by others and
by the family members themselves—has many such positions, and accompanying each is a special cultural content
and identification. To have a certain religious status means
that the child learns particular prayers and rituals; it
means also that he is identified with one particular group,
distinct from others. To have a father who is a farmer or
a doctor means that a given cultural content is passed on
to the child; it also means a certain occupational identity.
A similar situation exists for such statuses as race, social
class, family name, nationality, and ethnic affiliation. The
case of Johnny Rocco pointedly illustrates the importance
of family reputation:

> Johnny hadn't been running the streets long when the
> knowledge was borne in on him that being a Rocco made
> him "something special"; the reputation of the notorious
> Roccos, known to neighbors, schools, police, and welfare
> agencies as "chiselers, thieves, and trouble-makers," pre-
> ceded him. The cop on the beat, Johnny says, always had
> some cynical smart crack to make. . . . Certain children
> were not permitted to play with him. Wherever he went—
> on the streets, in the neighborhood, settlement house, at
> the welfare agency's penny milk station, at school, where

other Roccos had been before him—he recognized himself by a gesture, an oblique remark, a wrong laugh.[3]

The parents, through their decisions, are partially responsible for the manner in which community and institutional forces impinge on the child. The parents decide where to live, where the family goes on vacation, whom the child may invite to the house, and often to which evening programs the TV set is tuned. Moreover, the family inevitably interprets this wider community to the child, passing judgment on institutions, neighbors, programs, and local group activities.

In any family, some of the behavior patterns that the child learns are characteristic of the larger culture, others are unique to the particular family. That the parents offer food and drink to guests is common to the culture; that they say "topsy" to mean bathroom is not; that the father goes to work is common; that he bakes cakes in his leisure time is not. Only when the child establishes relationships with other people and enlarges his outlook can he attain a relative perspective and learn the range of ways in which status behavior may be acceptably expressed.

The Family as an Interaction Structure. Although the family, in some respects, should be viewed as a unit, it is in other respects more usefully conceived as a structure of complex interaction patterns. For each member there are different expectations of behavior and each, through his position and participation, has a unique role in socialization.

Each person's participations include many types of behavior, both in and out of the family. The mother prepares meals for the family, dresses the children, attends club meetings, writes Christmas cards, packs for holiday trips, gossips with neighboring housewives, and takes care of the child who is ill. The father serves drinks to guests, writes checks, washes the car, consoles the mother when she is upset, puts up curtain rods, attends business conventions, and takes part in numerous activities on his job.

These various behaviors can be classified under particular status headings: the mother, depending on her activity and the perspective, is woman, wife, clubwoman, shopper, neighbor, church member, and daughter; the father is husband, host, office worker, handyman, lodge member, and home owner.

Each child too has his statuses. He may be son, eldest child, schoolboy, club member, pet owner, choir singer, member of a football team, and camper—each implying certain types of role behavior. The particular details vary with such characteristics as age, sex, health, capabilities, and family socio-economic level.

Each status, we have observed, may be expressed in many different ways and with many different sentiments. Parents may be more or less expressive of their feelings, more or less authoritative, more or less protective. The mother, in dressing a young child, may demand or plead for his cooperation; the father in disciplining the child may be angry or businesslike. When the sentiments are typical of the larger culture group to which the family belongs, the child is more likely to take them for granted; when the sentiments are atypical, the child is apt to be conscious of his family's uniqueness.

The child learns values, sentiments, and status expectations through experiences with each member of the family. In a family with one child, there are three two-person relationships—father and mother, father and child, mother and child; in a family of five persons, there are ten two-person relationships; in a family of seven, twenty-one. The number of potential relationships in a family with three children, considering relationships between two persons and those between any one and combinations of two or more others, is sixty-five. This numerical factor, in itself, inevitably affects the particular character of emotional relations, cliques, and authority patterns. For example, in a family with one child—which serves as the model for the Oedipus complex—the emotional ties are likely to be concentrated, with resulting extreme jealousies. The presence of numerous brothers and sisters tends to obviate this particular problem, although at the same time it creates others.[4]

In the family, as in any small group, patterns develop, and each individual comes to have a unique relationship with each other individual. The choice of topics of conversation, the manner of responding to requests, the reaction to a family member's stroke of good fortune, the type of humor—all vary depending on the particular relationship between the parties. The child's mother may berate him when he dirties his new clothes; his father may permit him to use the electric drill; his brother may initiate him into types of horseplay. If he tells a *risqué* story, his father reacts in one way, his mother in another, and his brother in still another. His father plays more roughly with him than he does with baby brother or the neighbor's son; his mother demands different tasks of him than of his sister. He observes as well the unique relationships of others. His mother discusses party dresses only with his sister, and his father wrangles about family finances only with his mother. It is through such experiences that the child becomes familiar with a range of emotional relationships and gains a knowledge of the status expectations of boy, girl, spouse, and children of different birth order.

Mechanisms. The mechanisms of socialization are of special importance in the family. The child's first rewards and punishments, first image of himself, and first models of behavior are experienced in the family setting, and all help to develop a "personality base," subject to subsequent influences. The child's reaction to others is partially determined by his previous relationships with parents and siblings.[5] The late Harry Stack Sullivan suggested that early family experiences are often quite subtle, and that, almost from birth, the mother, through empathy, communicates to the child such sentiments as love, hate, confidence, anxiety, and fear—all of which have a long-run effect on personality.[6] And, as we have observed, personality type is closely related to the socialization process itself.

In the socialization of the child, members of his family use every technique and device that we have cited. They instruct, guide, respond to the child's actions, and bring him into their activities. Everyday behavior is especially important in showing the child the patterns and sentiments characteristic of his group. Dressing a child up when guests are expected suggests the importance of a family "front" and family solidarity.[7] Attending a wedding suggests behavior and feelings suitable to the occasion. Casual remarks about carpenters or painters working in the house may suggest that this occupation is an unworthy vocation for a son.

The child, on his part, generally just "picks up" appropriate patterns and values. He observes, participates with others, plays at roles, and judges his own thoughts and behavior. Moreover, merely through emotional identification with his parents, be the occasion sad, happy, embarrassing, or annoying, he comes to know and experience many appropriate sentiments. Claudia Lewis gives a good illustration of this process in describing a funeral for a baby in Tennessee mountain country:

> The room was filled with neighbors who had come to sit with the bereaved family . . . small children from the neighborhood felt free to wander in and out . . . two neighbor women . . . lifted the body . . . and laid it in the coffin. Everyone crowded around, children and all. . . . Up at the graveyard the coffin was opened. . . . All of the people . . . wept miserably. I noticed that four or five curious little boys had crowded up close to the open coffin, and were standing there solemnly staring at what must have been a somewhat terrifying sight.[8]

In their direct contact with the child, parents reward and punish. If the child behaves as they desire, he may be complimented, invited to participate, or given a prize; if he behaves otherwise, he may be slapped, shouted at, ignored, deprived of something he wishes, or accused of disappointing them. Parents thus indicate to the child that he cannot always behave as he pleases and that he should adhere to certain standards. Middle-class parents often

suggest—explicitly or implicitly—that the child who sup-
presses or defers his immediate gratifications will be rewarded in the future.[9] If he saves his money, he will earn
enough to buy a bicycle; if he shares a toy with his
brother, he will get a new one; if he obeys his parents, he
will receive better Christmas presents.

In the earliest months of life, a child may conform to
the wishes of his parents merely to gain their approval
and avoid punishment. Once he develops a self, in the
sense discussed in Chapter 3, and has the ability to view
his own behavior, he can better understand the demands
that are made of him and make more rapid strides in
socialization. With a self, he becomes aware of his statuses
and has guides for his behavior. His parents, for example,
view him as a potential scholar. Internalizing their view
of him, he too sees himself as a scholar and he can now
know the appropriate models and membership groups for
this particular status. This same principle may be applied
to delinquent behavior. The parents, for whatever reason,
view the child as a "bad boy." Adopting the parents'
image, the child sees himself as a "bad boy" and thereby
plays the appropriate part and looks for appropriate
models.

With self-awareness the child also becomes potentially
more independent of his limited family perspective.
Through contradictions within the family and contacts outside the home, he becomes more conscious of his family's
and his own distinctive ways. Since the standards by
which he judges himself may come to differ from those
of his parents, he can justify more independent action.
Further, he can take the position of outside groups, with
other standards, and judge his own family. In Herman
Lantz's study of a coal-mining town, he quotes the comment of an upper-class resident:

> When I was growing up I felt ashamed of [my mother]
> because she was so attractive and did not wear long dresses
> and black hose like the miners' wives did. . . . You see,
> the miners' kids were proud of their families and if your
> family didn't fit the pattern they r ally let you know about

it. The kids would draw off in their own group to say something about the mines or else the union and this was considered a secret and not for the ears of us other children.[10]

Thus, as the child makes use of his self, the significance to him of his parents' behavior changes considerably.

Socialization into Sex Roles. Consideration of socialization into sex roles should help to clarify the functions of the family. No adult role is more fundamental in any society: "If any of us were dropped by parachute into . . . the midst of an unknown tribe, the very first observation to be made about us would concern our sex." [11] Many agencies share in teaching a child the expected behavior of his sex, but the family is pre-eminent.

The girl is to be socialized into the role of woman, the boy into the role of man. In our society, the most common pattern for the woman, following her schooling, is to take an appropriate job, marry, and perhaps continue to work until she has children. Her primary tasks then are to manage the home and care for the children. For the man, the job is more important; it remains the source of family income and the primary determinant of the family's socio-economic position.

Differences exist in expressive behavior, interests, and popular image. Men walk, talk, light matches, and cross their knees differently from women. Men are more concerned with sports and politics; women with fashions and beauty products. Men are considered to be more rugged and to speak more coarsely; women to be more sentimental and disposed to cry.

Leaving aside the influence of hereditary dispositions— and there is no consensus on their relative significance —boys and girls come to learn their sex identities and expectations of behavior through differential observations, treatment, and emotional attachments. The significant others may be explicit and say, "Johnny is a boy and should behave like one." More often the definitions and treatment are unreflective and matter-of-course. The girl is (or, at least, was until recently) given pink, the boy blue; the girl a doll carriage and the boy a baseball glove. The boy is told to be brave, is complimented for throwing a ball well, may be locked out of the room when his mother is dressing, and kidded about being a Momma's boy. The girl is told to keep her dress down, is laughed at —or commended—for flirting, is admired for her curls, and teased for acting like a tomboy. The child, in innumerable instances of everyday life, has his behavior defined in sex-status terms and, in some way or another, is rewarded for appropriate behavior and ignored or punished for inappropriate behavior.

Of central importance, especially for an appropriate sex identity, are the models of behavior which significant others present to the child. Men and women behave differently before the child, and treat him differently. Women kiss him, dress him, prepare his meals, and use "feminine" expressions in talking to him. Men shake his hand, handle him more roughly, play ball with him, and take him fishing. The various individuals and symbols held up for him to emulate are also sex identified—the boy is given a cowboy suit named after a western TV star or told to help around the house like the boy next door.

Learning a sex role is closely related to emotional attachments. An important problem for the boy is to emancipate himself from a dependency relationship with his mother and to identify or develop a "we" feeling with his father and other males. Since the boy in our society does not generally see his father at work, one significant dimension of the male model is often obscure. The story is told of the four-year-old boy playing "Daddy" who put on his hat and coat, said "Goodbye," and walked out of the front door, only to return a few minutes later because he didn't know what to do next. While employing his father as a sex status model, the boy must not become so closely identified that he wants to replace him in the immediate family—the danger of the Oedipus complex.[12] The complementary problems of the young girl have their own variations.

Sex identity and role behavior are inseparable from the development of the self. Once the child learns his sex status, he can view his own behavior from the position of others and judge whether or not he is behaving properly. Thus the boy knows he shouldn't be interested in dolls, and the girl knows she may acceptably cringe at the sight of an earthworm. Moreover, the boy and girl can know which are appropriate models and which are not and can anticipate their future adult sex statuses with their respective rights and duties. Most children also so internalize these expectations that they can develop romantic and sexual attachments to members of the opposite sex. Confusion and uncertainty about self-image and sex identity can become a basis for homosexual tendencies.

In recent years, considerable discussion has concerned the changing patterns of sex roles and the ambiguity of sex models. Urbanization, technical specialization, changing birth rates, the extension of education, the growth of the mass media, and a generally rising standard of living have all affected the behavior of men and women and the patterns of socialization. Paid baby-sitters have replaced grandparents; children may never see many of their cousins; new appliances and service industries give the housewife more time for other activities; women train for professional careers and compete with men for available jobs; movie and TV stars quickly become widely known.

For the child, these changes and trends may present a confused picture. We need only note several female models that are currently esteemed in our society—the professional career woman, traditional housewife, glamour girl, "pal," and active clubwoman. The young girl not only becomes aware of such varied heroines, but is herself rewarded for correspondingly varied types of behavior—attractiveness to boys, ability in school, leadership qualities, cooking, all-around friendliness, and efficiency on the job. A similar situation exists for the boy. Among the popular models are sports and entertainment stars, the duty-abiding agent of the law, the successful business or professional man, the scientist; and he too is rewarded for such different types of behavior as scholastic achievement, popularity with girls, club leadership, success in sports, and dutiful aid to the family.

With so many sex status symbols, parents and other socializing agents may be inconsistent or uncertain in the paths of development they encourage and the models they present. The child does not always know by which standards to judge himself and others. For some, the inconsistency of these images has undoubtedly made it difficult to develop harmonious and integrated heterosexual relationships.[13] On the other hand, one should not assume that apparently logically contradictory roles are actually experienced as such. One study suggests that college girls are sophisticated enough to be aware of contradictory demands, yet experience no particular confusion in deciding how to behave in specific instances. They have, to their own satisfaction, worked out a *modus vivendi*.[14] Perhaps at least some role confusion is a "normal" part of middle-class culture.

The School

The child in school has certain rights and obligations. He is expected to attend school, focus his attention on his studies, compare himself with his classmates, and participate in school activities. As he advances into higher grades, he is presumed to be capable of more complex participation, and his rights and obligations change accordingly.

Like the family, the school is a recognized institution representing the adult authority of the society. Unlike the family, the school is formalized with established rules, and, since the child is in a different class each year, does not ordinarily permit him to form enduring interpersonal ties with teachers. Although the trends of "progressive" education may suggest otherwise, the school also necessarily has a limited program and is never likely to be concerned with the "whole child."

The ties between school and family are close. Whether a child is receptive or has serious qualms when he enters school, whether he is prone to accept or reject the school authorities, how he reacts to the teachers as models of behavior—all, to a great degree, are a function of attitudes and orientations which have been developed in the family setting. The child attending school, moreover, remains a member of his family, and the two agencies may reinforce or counteract each others' influence—or both. Parents and teachers may jointly encourage homework, achievement, and respect for school authorities; or they may disagree about the merit of the instruction, importance of a foreign language, or value of extracurricular activities. A recent report on Soviet children illustrates the confusion that may stem from traditional doctrine of parents and scientific sex instruction of the school. Two kindergarten children are conversing:

—My mother has gone to Moscow to buy me a little sister.
—Silly, it's only in America that people buy children. Here they come out of the womb.
—That's untrue. In America, children are made by monkeys.[15]

Functions of the School. Manifestly, the school's socializing function is to "educate the young," that is, to transmit certain basic knowledge and skills of the culture. There are other less obvious functions. By providing other models of behavior and sources of knowledge, the school helps the child to gain emotional independence from his family. This development is gradual. In the early years, the teacher, usually a woman, is more like the mother and concerned with the general well-being of the child. She may temper criticisms or invidious comparisons that might be unduly upsetting and praise a backward student's scribbles as well as the creative drawings of his neighbor.

The school also functions as a "sorting and sifting" agency. It serves on the one hand to reinforce existing statuses of students and, on the other, to encourage upward mobility. Existing statuses are reinforced in part by controlled environments, the exclusive private school representing an extreme example. However, many schools have students relatively homogeneous in family income, occupational level, and ethnic affiliation; and, even where there is heterogeneity, the allocation of students into sections and peer group choices—sometimes aided and abetted by parents—have essentially the same result. Reinforcement of statuses also comes about through differential treatment by teachers and school authorities. Studies show, for example, that students of well-to-do families often have better facilities and a more advanced curriculum, and receive more encouragement and more lenient treatment than do children of lower income groups. To quote August B. Hollingshead's well-known study of Elmtown:

> . . . teachers do cater to the prominent families. . . . New teachers soon learn from their associations with other teachers, townspeople, parents, and adolescents "who is who" and what one should or should not do to avoid trouble. . . . Teachers, if they are successful, act judiciously in their relations with the children of the powerful; on appropriate occasions they look the other way.[16]

This, of course, is an incomplete picture. Those children who do well in school, whatever their family backgrounds, are likely to win awards, be encouraged by their teachers, go on to higher education, and become successful men and women in the community. There is some opportunity for the children of economically poor families to attain positions higher than those of their parents and, conversely, for children of well-to-do families to fail and drop into positions lower than those occupied by their parents. Several studies touch on varied aspects of this problem.[17]

The school functions further to reinforce values current in conventional society. As an agency guided by successful educators, and business and professional men, the school cannot be expected to represent any seriously rebellious or deviant ideas. The child learns much from the course work itself. He may be taught health lessons in which he is advised to wash his hands before eating. He may read a story in which a nurse risks her life to help people with contagious diseases or see a play in which the obedient, good son is rewarded and the disobedient, bad son is punished. Or perhaps the stories concern the behavior and images of doctors, stepmothers, princes, orphans, and soldiers. In early grades, the child may learn:

> Oh, it's hippety hop to bed.
> I'd rather stay up instead.
> But when father says "must,"
> There's nothing but just
> Go hippety hop to bed.

or

> Little Polly Flinders sat among the cinders
> Warming her pretty little toes.
> Her mother came and caught her
> And spanked her little daughter
> For spoiling her nice, new clothes.

Such songs require no "manipulation" on the part of the teacher to bring out the moral.

Often the values and status expectations in curriculum content are more subtle. The same *arithmetic* is learned if a problem asks, "How much interest does a man pay per annum if he borrows $1000 from the bank at 6 per cent interest?" or if it asks, "How many people are killed if a sudden Communist bomber attack kills 6 per cent of the population in a community of 1000 inhabitants?" The former illustration, besides teaching arithmetic, suggests the statuses of the borrower and banker and the acceptability of their transaction; the latter suggests negative attitudes towards Communist countries.

In like manner, the activities and organizational features of the school indicate status expectations and values. The child learns, through numerous comments of teachers, that he should be punctual, write legibly, not waste paper, and be quiet when the teacher is speaking. In club activities he learns the appropriate behavior of the club member, the prestige value of being an officer, and techniques of organizing club affairs. He learns in group games that he should take turns and play fairly; he learns in pep rallies and school festivities that he is expected to, and actually does, experience loyalty to his school and solidarity with other students. And finally, of course, through grades, promotions, and awards, and the approval that comes from doing well, the child learns the values of scholastic achievement and success. At least, that is the expectation; in reality, combinations of such factors as low grades, contrary decrees of the peer group, lack of interest by parents, and unpopular teachers may—especially for lower-class groups—implant opposite values and attitudes.

The Teacher as a Socializing Agent. Although a child's teachers in his early school years change from year to year and later from subject to subject, we may still speak in general terms of the teacher as a socializing agent. Teachers vary in their interests, types of humor, opinions about extracurricular activities, and so on, but there are some values and ideals that virtually all teachers represent and from which students cannot hope to escape. First, teachers of necessity stand for adult authority and the need for order and discipline. Second, they represent the values of knowledge and educational achievement, at least in their particular fields of instruction. And third, they represent such "middle-class" personality characteristics as correct speech, respect for public property, politeness, and neatness.

In the early school years, a child is likely to spend many hours a day with one teacher who, as suggested above, is concerned with his cooperation, health habits, deportment, effort, and other psychological and social aspects of his development. As the child advances in school, the demands of the teacher become more specific and focus on particular subjects. Achievement is stressed, and ideally the teacher judges the student only on the basis of his performance.[18] In reality, as we have noted, certain students, whether because of family background, athletic ability, especially pleasant personalities, or other circumstances, may be unduly favored.

Teachers probably are important socializing agents less because of what they teach than because of the models or significant others they become. Despite a popular depreciatory image of teachers, students are expected to defer to them and often in fact form strong emotional attachments to teachers. The significance of the teacher as a model may range from the relatively trivial to the extremely influential. The student may merely adopt a favorite phrase or voice inflection, or he may look up to the teacher as a hero ideal, worthy of admiration and emulation. The greatest influence of the teacher probably derives from the establishment of a sponsor-protégé relationship. W. Lloyd Warner and James C. Abegglen, in their study of business leaders, point out that many upwardly mobile executives were encouraged and aided by older men and these "men seem most often to have been teachers." [19] Athletic coaches are also cited. With reference to the family, Warner and Abegglen report that these sponsors often served as father-figures when the students' own fathers were ineffective or objects of hostility.

Teachers do not become important models for all students. One relevant variable is social class. Although the upper-class student may like and respect a particular teacher, he is likely to view him as a social inferior and not someone he might himself become. On the contrary, the working-class pupil is more apt to look up to the teacher as a direct model for later life. Many students— 44 per cent in one recent study in Texas[20]—have employed the teaching profession as a means of moving up the social scale.

Mechanisms. The previously described mechanisms of socialization are also evident in the school. School authorities seek to motivate the child by giving conditional approval, rewarding and punishing according to his behavior and performance. Also, consciously or unconsciously, they cite models of behavior for the child and become models themselves.

Compared to the family, the rewards of the school situation—grades, promotions, permission to participate in certain activities, compliments, and leadership positions—are quite formalized. There are particular age-grade expectations with specific tasks and standards, and the child is judged by the degree to which he measures up to these expectations. Almost inevitably there are rankings and comparisons with other students.

In disciplining and teaching the child, the school authorities may use the child's dependence on his family and peer group. The child's mother may be "asked" to see the principal or, often more effectively, the child may be shamed before his fellow students. Such techniques of course are effective only if the family and peer group in some way support the school.

The pupil on his part learns the patterns of the school system and, to some unmeasurable degree, those of the society at large. He consciously studies certain subjects; he observes what happens in school to himself, his fellow students, and the authorities; he participates in various activities and experiences accompanying feelings. In order to know what is expected and desired of him, he also imaginatively takes the position of his teachers. In addition, as we have observed, the child may develop an emotional attachment to a teacher ranging from a specific situation to a strong identification with him as a hero ideal.

The Peer Group

The social organization of the child's peer group* is quite different from that of the family and school. First of all, the peer group, by definition, is made up of members who

* For purposes of analysis, we have rather sharply distinguished between the peer group and the school system. The peer group, of course, operates within as well as without the school system.[21]

have about the same age status. Within the peer group, the members are differently ranked and have varying degrees of power; however, *vis-a-vis* the established authority figures, they have roughly the same positions.

There is another important difference too: the peer group is centered about its own immediate concerns. Adult authority figures instruct the child in traditional norms and values with an awareness that the child must learn to function in the ongoing society. The peer group, without authority figures recognized as such by adult society, has no such responsibilities, and any long-run socializing implications are unintentional and accidental.

Nor is the peer group usually an established institutional structure with traditional statuses and established forms. It has its customs and organization, but ordinarily the rights and duties of each member are less well defined and the members may more readily modify old patterns. For groups of younger children (or even for "delinquent gangs" [22]) without specialized interests, it may not even be clear in what respects someone is or is not a member.

The child, as he develops and moves in changing circles, ordinarily participates in a succession of peer groups. He may also be a member of several peer groups simultaneously—a circle of cousins, cliques in the neighborhood, school, church, summer camp, and so on. For each group to which he belongs, he has the status of group member with its accompanying expectations of thought and behavior. As a new member of an ongoing group, a child is socialized into its patterns; as an established member, he helps socialize others and evolve new patterns.

Functions of the Peer Group. The peer group has certain distinctive functions in socializing the child, some of which cannot be fulfilled easily, if at all, by such enduring and fixed structures as the family and school. First, the peer group gives the child experience in egalitarian types of relationships. In the established institutions, the parties are of different authority and power, differences which often lead to frustration and hostile reactions on the part of those who are subordinate. The so-called "democratic family" or "democratic school" in which children and adults are equally responsible for making basic decisions is more myth than reality.

Second, since institutions ordinarily represent the established order and conventional values of the culture, they are likely to avoid teaching "taboo" subjects. Or, if they do attempt to teach in these areas, they may do so in a relatively formal and forced manner. Such is the case in our own society with respect to sex education. The importance of the peer group is suggested in the not atypical experience of a boy in a coal mining town who writes:

Sex was taboo at home. Sex education came from the older boys, picked up around the playgrounds, shows, pool halls, and not a little from the inscriptions on the walls of public toilets. It was learned more practically wherever boys and girls got together. It was made sordid and the butt of many jokes and pranks.[23]

Another comment by a girl of about ten illustrates how early in life attitudes and emotions about sex develop:

Bee is too much like a pig. . . . She talks about boys all the time. Talks dirty about them. She hangs around boys in and out of school. She uses nasty words and tells dirty jokes. . . . Boys don't know what she's like.[24]

Sex education is not limited to the peer group; it is ramified through the family, biology courses, movies, advertisements, the church, and, of course, direct experience. Robert Dubin, in discussing the relationship between deviant behavior and social structure, points out that some types of sexual behavior, although legal and legitimate, still require private experimentation since instruction is so awkward and embarrassing.[25]

Third, if the society is rapidly changing, authority figures may not always have sufficient knowledge to teach the child current fashions and trends, and the task may be performed, at least in part, by peer groups. This doesn't apply to science and politics, but it does often apply to songs, dances, sports, and other aspects of the popular culture. To the members of the peer group, the older generation may be "old fogies," "ancients," or "just not hep."

The peer group serves further to expand the social horizons of the child and to make him a more complex person. He experiences different feelings and becomes familiar with new games, codes, and interests. The child has a testing ground for the ideas and characteristics that he has previously learned and developed. His ideas of cleanliness, his "cute shy" manner in telling stories, his techniques for getting what he wants—all may receive very different reactions from the peer group than from the family. Whether or not the child continues to have particular characteristics, or how and when he expresses them, depends on many factors; however, at the very minimum, he learns that certain standards are variable, and, in the peer group, he views and judges himself from a more complex perspective. A vivid example of this situation is found in W. Somerset Maugham's *Of Human Bondage.* "Philip" was born with a club foot and has until now received considerable sympathy because of it. When he arrives at school, his classmates taunt him:

> One of them had the brilliant idea of imitating Philip's clumsy run. Other boys saw it and began to laugh . . . they ran around Philip, limping grotesquely, screaming in their treble voices with shrill laughter. . . . One of them invented an odd, rolling limp that struck the rest as supremely ridiculous, and several of the boys lay down on the ground and rolled about in laughter. Philip . . . could not make out why they were laughing at him.[26]

Finally, through the peer group, the child can become more independent of his parents and other authorities. In the peer group, he develops new emotional ties and identifies with new models. He seeks the attention, acceptance, or good will of peer group members and views himself according to the group's standards. Success in sports, dancing ability, sexual exploits, and so on, perhaps quite unimportant to his family, now become primary considerations in his self-image. In extreme cases, these new standards may become linked to hostile feelings towards all conventional authority figures and lead to deliberately provocative and defiant behavior. Albert Cohen uses this idea as a part of his theory of a delinquent subculture:

> [Throughout the delinquent's repertoire] there is a kind of *malice* apparent, an enjoyment in the discomfiture of others, a delight in the defiance of taboos itself. . . . There is a keen delight in terrorizing "good" children, in driving them from playgrounds and gyms. . . . The same spirit is evident in playing hookey and in misbehavior in school. The teacher and her rules are not merely something onerous to be evaded. They are to be *flouted*. There is an element of active spite and malice, contempt and ridicule, challenge and defiance.[27]

The peer group in this way may serve as a comforting collective cushion in the face of demands of authority. On the other hand, for the spurned child, these same group ties may greatly increase his sense of social isolation. In *The Member of the Wedding,* Carson McCullers effectively portrays Frankie's sensitivity to rejection by the peer group:

> "Look," John Henry said, and he was staring out of the window. "I think those big girls are having a party in their clubhouse."

> "Hush!" Frankie screamed suddenly. "Don't mention those crooks to me."

> There was in the neighborhood a clubhouse, and Frankie was not a member. . . . Frankie knew all of the club members, and until this summer she had been like a younger member of their crowd, but now they had this club and she was not a member. They had said she was too young and too mean. On Saturday night she could hear the terrible music and see from far away their light. Sometimes she went around to the alley behind the clubhouse and stood near a honeysuckle fence. She stood in the alley and watched and listened. They were very long, those parties.

"Maybe they will change their mind and invite you," John Henry said.

"The son-of-a-bitches." [28]

Culture of the Peer Group. The peer group has its own patterns of thought and behavior, patterns which sometimes seem to be almost unlimited in content. Five-year-olds play different games from fifteen-year-olds; boys talk differently from girls; slum children dress differently from wealthy children.

The culture which the peer group transmits to the child includes norms and values. An adolescent gang may have customary ways of greeting and of behaving on dates; and it may highly value ability in basketball and popularity with a certain clique of girls. The culture may include definitions of other groups and other elements of the environment. A certain kind of music is "cool," another is "for the squares"; certain popular singers are acceptable idols, while most political figures are beyond the realm of legitimate interest. The culture may include symbols which identify and distinguish the group—uniforms, nicknames, insignia—and also a general image of the peer group itself, of its distinguishing characteristics, special interests, and neighborhood or institutional loyalties.

Some of these culture patterns and interests of the peer group are fashions or fads. Special slang expressions, items of clothing, and dance steps are soon replaced by others. Other patterns may persist for many years, with appropriate socialization of each new generation. Thus fraternities have songs, rituals, and traditional rivalries which are passed on to each new member. In certain deteriorated sections of Chicago, Clifford Shaw suggests, delinquent patterns had been passed down through successive generations of peer groups, even when the ethnic composition of the groups changed;[29] and certain children's songs and games have persisted for centuries, passed on by successive generations of children.[30]

Mechanisms. Socialization in peer groups is taught to and picked up by new members in the course of interaction.

The new member is interested in the companionship, attention, or good will of the group or of those members of the group who are significant for him, and the group is in a position to satisfy this interest. For behaving in the appropriate or valued manner, the group rewards its members by bestowing attention, approval, or leadership, or by giving permission to participate or to employ certain symbols. For behaving otherwise, the peer group punishes by disdain, ostracism, or other expressions of disapproval. As with other socializing agencies, the child comes to view himself as an object from the point of view of the group, and to internalize its standards. While he is a member, these standards are reinforced by the feelings of solidarity and support that he obtains from others.

The peer group also socializes by providing models. Within the peer group, the members have different positions and some, for whatever reason, may become especially significant as models of identification. It is they whose good will is sought and to whose behavior and ideas the child is particularly responsive. The peer group may also define other models. For example, in fan clubs, particular movie stars or popular singers are revered and the members may model their own behavior after them or evaluate others by their reputed characteristics.

It is impossible to know precisely what characteristics are "permanently" internalized as a result of peer group experience; too many contingent factors are present, both in the peer group and in the life of the developing child. At one extreme, a child's other social attachments may be so strong that the socializing effect of the peer group is minimal; at the other extreme, the support of the peer group may be so significant that its perspective becomes all-important and the child may risk virtual excommunication from other groups. Much depends on the relationship between the values of the peer group and the values of other agencies. Contrast the attitude of a slum group which scoffs at scholastic achievement:

> His gang teaches him to fear being taken in by the teacher, of being a softie with her. To study homework seriously is

literally a disgrace. Instead of boasting of good marks in school, one conceals them, if he ever receives any.[31]

with the remarks of a middle-class suburban high school boy:

You would be surprised just how much [school work] counts for boys. I was at a party last year after I came first in the class. I could just stand there and not say a word all evening. Everybody came up to me and all that kind of stuff. Just because I came first in the class, I was the "brain" for the evening.[32]

David Riesman in *The Lonely Crowd* suggests that peer groups have become much more significant in socialization among upper social strata than they were a few generations ago. Formerly a child was more likely to become "inner-directed," to internalize definitive standards of thought and behavior which he upheld throughout his life. He might develop hardfast standards of right and wrong or idiosyncratic hobbies, and whether or not others behaved similarly or approved of his way of life was not important. In recent years, however, the trend has been towards "other-direction," towards following the standards of the immediate peer group. As the morals and hobbies of the immediate groups vary, so do those of the particular child. A person may differ from others in minor respects—he may like Teresa Brewer more than Dinah Shore or prefer basketball to football—but major differences are not condoned. The basic goal upheld by parents as well as peers is to be well adjusted. Riesman writes:

The adults . . . are concerned with his "adjustment." They, too, tend to ignore and even suppress invisible differences between their children and the children of others. . . . The effort is to cut everyone down to size who stands up or stands out in any direction. Beginning with the very young and going on from there, overt vanity is treated as one of the worst offenses. . . . All "knobby" or idiosyncratic qualities and vices are more or less eliminated or repressed.[33]

The trend to other-direction, Riesman suggests, is evidenced in many areas of life—"manipulation" by parents, in "progressive education," in the selection of executives in industry, the political choices of voters, and the stories and popular heroes of the mass media.

The Media of Mass Communication

The media of mass communication comprise the press, radio, magazines, comic booklets, movies, television, and other means of communication which reach large heterogeneous audiences and in which there is an impersonal medium between the sender and receiver.[34] In contrast to other agencies, the mass media are a relatively recent development and do not directly involve interpersonal interaction; nevertheless, they are a significant agency of socialization. First of all, the content and personnel of the mass media, as evidenced in motion pictures and movie stars, have considerable interest and prestige value in the society at large. Second, as demonstrated particularly by advertising, the mass media can be very effective in their influence. Third, the mass media, especially in recent years, have become part of the child's world when he is still a baby and, as he gets older, take up many hours of his day. And finally, the mass media portray many characteristics of popular culture, for example, of romance and types of humor, which other agencies often do not transmit.

Since they include such a range of materials, the mass media cannot always be viewed from a single perspective. In content, *The New York Times,* a comedy television show, a soap-opera, and a science-fiction comic booklet do not have much in common. Nor can the mass media be considered in isolation. They are ordinarily seen or heard in group settings, and the family and peer group have a considerable influence in guiding exposure to, and generally defining, their content. The significance of the mass media is generally to be found not in the media themselves, but in the link between them and interpersonal relationships.

Themes and Implications of Mass Media Content. The mass media, by their content alone, teach many of the ways of the society. This is evident in the behavior we take for granted—the duties of the detective, waitress, or sheriff; the functions of the hospital, advertising agency, and police court; behavior in a night club or airplane; the language of the prison, army, or courtroom; the relationships between nurses and doctors or secretaries and their bosses. Such settings and relationships are portrayed time and again in films, television shows, comic strips, and radio programs, and all "teach"—however misleadingly —norms, status positions, and institutional functions.

The recurrent themes and story types also suggest appropriate values and ideals for particular status positions. The Western story form, for example, assumes that a law enforcement officer fights for justice and that men who dishonestly seek wealth are evil; the romantic musical implies that love, rather than wealth, makes a girl happy, and that the world of showfolk is exciting and glamorous; the radio serial suggests that it is praiseworthy for a housewife to help people with emotional problems and that a man should be wary of a woman who capitalizes solely on her "sex."

The mass media also present models of behavior—of heroes, villains, and comics, of occupational, ethnic, and personality types. The Western hero, for example, although sometimes rather foolish and sadistic, is neat, courageous, and self-reliant, and does not fight unfairly or lose his temper; the crime-investigator model is honest, serious, and devoted to his job; the light comedy musical heroine is pleasant, moral, attractive to men, and capable of romantic feelings; the doctor is serious, efficient, available in emergencies, and concerned with the welfare of his patients.

Socializing Influence of the Mass Media. Through continual exposure to the recurrent aspects of the mass media

—reinforced at times by peer groups, teachers, "live" entertainment, and other agencies—a child gains a knowledge of story plots, ways of life, and social types which extends far beyond his immediate experience and relationships. Teachers at the Oak Lane Country Day School in Philadelphia cite the following illustrations:

> During a fourth grade social studies class the children were talking about prehistoric animals . . . several children asked how anything could be known about creatures who lived before the days of written records. One student gave a full and vivid account of a television program she had recently seen . . . about an archaeologist who had dug up and assembled the bones of an animal judged to be prehistoric.

> Two four-year-old boys found a worm on the playground. The children compared it to a snake and one of the boys told of a TV program . . . about large rattlesnakes that live in the desert. "Even the man couldn't touch those snakes," he said, "because they were poison. See, I can hold the worm, it's not poison." [35]

How much socializing influence the mass media have is not clear, although undoubtedly it is extensive. Sometimes, they can apparently change attitudes towards given groups. In one of a series of pioneer studies in the early 1930s, Peterson and Thurstone found that a group of white children, on an average, thought less well of Negroes after seeing the strongly anti-Negro film *Birth of a Nation* than they had before.[36] If many related films are shown, the effects are even greater. It also seems plausible that concerted efforts by the mass media can direct a group's attitudes and sentiments, especially when no contrary expressions are permitted, as in Nazi Germany or Soviet Russia.[37] However, where counter influences exist or where the audience has a deep-seated resistance to the message, the efforts of the "persuaders" may boomerang. One study, for example, suggests that cartoon propaganda sympathetic to minority groups had if anything a negative influence, rather than that intended, on a group of prejudiced subjects;[38] another found that a blood donor campaign among college students which stressed competition between campus groups and ignored humanitarian objectives considerably annoyed many of the students.[39]

The mass media also function to give the child a wider range of role-taking models than he ordinarily finds in his family, neighborhood, and school. Movie and television stars, for example, who are "typed" to represent given status and personality characteristics, become public symbols. As such, they may be used by the child as sources of imitation and role playing. At most, they become strong objects of hero worship and identification; at the very least, they indicate to the child that there are other standards of behavior besides those of his immediate environment.[40] What influence a movie or TV star has in a specific case depends not only on the characteristics he symbolizes, but also on his definition by others and the personality of the particular child.

The problems concerning the socializing influence of the mass media are complex. First, the child's reactions depend on his level of development. Katherine M. Wolf and Marjorie Fiske, in a study of the reading of comics among children, suggest that there is a self-selection according to age. Children below ten like the "funny animal" comics in which animals go to school, enjoy a home life, and in other ways behave plausibly. Children at eleven and twelve more often prefer adventure comics in which invincible "superman" types fly from planet to planet or use X-ray vision. Children over thirteen more often prefer the "educational" comics with realistic settings and plausible behavior of historical or literary characters.[41] A recent study of television in England generally supports these results. The interest in children's programs—puppets, nature study, animal shows—is at its height at ages eight and nine, while older children prefer thrillers.[42]

Second, the particular preferences and reactions of the child depend upon his interpersonal relationships. Matilda and John Riley report that the young child who is oriented primarily to his family is more likely to prefer animal comics and programs of violence than is the child who is

oriented strongly to his peer group. In discussing older
boys, they suggest similarly that peer group members relate adventure story heroes to their everyday lives while
non-peer group members interpret these same heroes to
have invincible or even superhuman qualities.[43]

Finally, the selective perception and influence of themes
and heroes are related to social background. The authors
of one study, reporting on reactions to the film *Tomorrow
the World,* suggest that children of a Los Angeles slum
area, accustomed to disorder and violence, react differently
to this story of attempted murder than do children, largely
middle-class and Mormon, from Salt Lake City. The slum
children accept the aggression of the twelve-year-old Nazi-
trained boy as appropriate for a "gangster" type; the Salt
Lake City children are shocked.[44]

Mechanisms. Since the child ordinarily employs the mass
media for his immediate gratification and not to learn the
patterns of the society, the socialization which derives
therefrom is generally incidental. The mechanisms of
socialization of the mass media are unique in that there
is no direct personal interaction with the child. The media
in themselves do not punish, reward, love, hate, necessitate
day-to-day adjustments, or respond to feelings and actions.
In the mass media, the child sees or hears many situations
which are of only passing interest and seemingly of little
direct relevance to his own present or prospective way of
life. Only those situations and models which are used
imaginatively or directly in interaction situations become
of particular significance in socialization.

If a girl models her hair style after that of a TV star,
she is likely to be interested less in the style itself than in
her ongoing personal relationships with boys and girls. If
a child wants a cowboy suit after he sees a Western film,
one relevant factor is apt to be the anticipated reaction of
others. If a child is especially interested in crime stories,
he may imaginatively experience situations in which characters play heroic roles, gain prestige, receive rewards,

and participate in emotional situations—all of which are related to his everyday life.

It is not only the content of the mass media which is of interpersonal relevance; mere exposure to the mass media may be significant. A child may know that his parents disapprove of comic books or certain popular singers, and this knowledge in itself enters into his thought and behavior. Or he may know which programs are popular among his friends and use this information as a device for arousing interest or affirming leadership. Riesman writes:

> My interviews showed that each age group within a limited region and class had its own musical taste. . . . Within this general trend a girl might decide that she could not *stand* Vaughn Monroe or that Perry Como was tops. If she expressed herself so forcibly in detail, the chances were that she was, or wanted to be, an opinion leader.[45]

In these instances, when the child uses the mass media, he is viewing himself from the position of others and his relationship to them. Thus the child observes the mass media, imaginatively participates in them, and uses the characters as models; however, they must still be tested and applied in his interpersonal relationships.

We have discussed the major agencies of socialization; others, too, may be of great significance, depending on the child and the particular conditions of his life. The church, for example, although less important in modern America than in rural French Canada or Puritan New England, may still be instrumental in teaching a child to distinguish the sacred from the profane and in instilling feelings of group solidarity. Community agencies, such as Y.M.C.A.s and Boys' Clubs, may have a marked influence, especially insofar as they help widen the outlook of ethnic and lower-class children. The summer camp, particularly for middle-class children who attend every year from age three through adolescence, may be important for relation-

ships both with peers and authority figures. Nor is the
community itself to be ignored, since, with its distinctive
characteristics—industrial or resort, wealthy or poor, farm
or urban—it limits and guides the observations and participations of the child.

These agencies function to weaken the child's ties with
his family, give him new statuses, teach him different perspectives, and broaden his range of experience. Their
sanctions range from a denial of the use of facilities to
threats about the supernatural; their models vary from
group heroes to sympathetic but manipulating "big brothers."

In the experience of any particular child, the agencies
of socialization are closely interlinked. The child cannot
so compartmentalize his life that each agency remains
apart from others. Presumably the child assimilates the
"residues" of his experiences with the varied agencies into
his personality structure.

From these agencies, the child has learned a particular
cultural content. However, the content varies greatly;
depending on his group affiliations in the social structure,
he has been socialized into certain subcultural patterns
and not into others. This is the aspect of socialization to
which we now turn.

5 SOCIALIZATION AND SUBCULTURAL PATTERNS

Many elements characterize our North American culture and the experiences we have in common, including our clothes, foods, tools, advertisements, kitchen appliances, drugstore displays, popular sports, and entertainment heroes. Side by side with these common elements is diversity. Many economic, social, regional, and occupational groups, each with its distinctive characteristics, comprise our complex world.

To the child becoming socialized, these social differentiations are likely to be abstractions for, in his own experience, they are all closely intertwined. For one child, there may be a cultural complex which comprises distinct characteristics of New England, urban, male, Anglo-Saxon, upper class, private school, and corporation finance; for another the complex may be Southern, rural, female, Negro, lower class, country school, and farm labor; for still another it may be Midwestern, urban, male, Greek-Orthodox, parochial school, and independent small business.

Nevertheless each differentiation cuts through society and each has significant characteristics in common. Discussed below are three of the most important of these differentiations—those of social class, ethnic group, and community, particularly suburban, residence.

77

Social Class

Although social class is variously defined in social science literature, all social scientists recognize that there are socio-economic strata in the society and that different groups possess unequal amounts of wealth, influence, prestige, and "life chances." That the public also is not indifferent to social class is shown by the annoyance someone feels when he is judged to be of a class lower than that in which he places himself. Even children, when still of primary school age, are aware of class differences in behavior and evaluate others on the basis of class identification. One investigator, in a study of a New England industrial town, reports that children between the fourth and sixth grades begin to distinguish such symbols of social class as evening dress, delivering groceries, and riding horseback clothed in a riding habit; and by the eighth grade, adult stereotypes of social class are quite generally known.[1] Another sociologist, studying children aged ten to twelve in "Jonesville," a city in the Midwest, found that children of the upper middle class were generally judged by their classmates to be better looking and fairer playing than lower-class children, differences which were objectively unlikely.[2]

Social Class as a Way of Life. From the point of view of socialization, perhaps the most important aspect of social stratification is a group's "way of life." There are many "ways of life" associated with social class, ranging from a very small "upper upper" class with its genealogy, mansions, servants, yachts, debutantes, and private school education down to the déclassé. For purposes of illustration and contrast, in this section we shall focus on socialization in two class groups—one, the so-called "upper middle class," consisting primarily of families of well-to-do professional and businessmen, and the other, the "lower class," consisting primarily of families of unskilled laborers. Our "lower class" is not the stable working population, but rather the small proportion at the "ragged bottom," without steady incomes, living in slums, sharing a bathroom and kitchen, and often wearing used clothing.

Differences between the two groups exist in numerous areas of everyday life, in physical surroundings, language, manners, dress, entertainment, associations, expressions of sentiment, and institutional activities. The child in the upper middle class has his own bed, room, and clothes; he is never without food, clothing, light, or heat; he is taught to wash behind his ears and to keep his shoes shined; he is told not to carry mud onto the carpets; he learns to be mannerly at the table and to say "thank you," "please," "may I," "yes," and "he and I"; he tells his parents whom he sees and how he spends his time; he is accustomed to seeing cleaning women and baby-sitters. In contrast, the child of the lower class shares his room, bed, and clothes; he does not always have the "basic necessities of life"; he is permitted to go around with dirty hands and face; he may put his feet on a chair without censure; he says "can I," "ain't," "yeah," and "me and him"; he is relatively unconcerned with table manners or proper color combinations for his clothes; he never eats dinner at expensive restaurants; he rarely reports the details of his activities to his parents, and he lives a generally less protected life. The upper-middle-class child not only learns the behavior patterns of his family's status, he also learns and internalizes the accompanying values of cleanliness, privacy, respect for property, correct language forms, restraint at the table, and other proprieties. The lower-class child may also come to know and recognize these values, but for him they represent a world and way of life of which he is not a part.

In upper-middle-class groups, greater stress is also placed on the control of violence and aggression. The boy is admonished not to swear or be loud and rough, to fight only in self-defense, never to strike a girl, and to respect teachers and other authority figures. In contrast, in the world of the lower-class child, the able fighter is esteemed and violence is a more acceptable means of resolving disputes. A slum child writes:

As a kid I was always treated as a regular guy, because I
always split everything I had but mostly because I was
more or less a leader to them and could lick nearly every
one of them. I was often made fun of because I was fat,
but when I caught them they thought twice before razzing
me again.

This school was pretty tough; by that I mean the guys that
went to it. I am a pretty good mixer, if I say so myself,
and in two weeks I was one of the gang and known as
plenty tough.[3]

Sex too, except for common taboos on such practices
as incest and homosexuality, is viewed and practiced differently by the two groups. Members of the upper middle
class are more apt to accept masturbation, heavy petting,
and free sex play for the married, while proscribing relations with prostitutes or premarital sex relations. For
many lower-class persons, on the contrary, premarital sex
relations are normal, visiting prostitutes is acceptable, sex
play between spouses is more limited, and masturbation and
heavy petting are considered to be perverse. Each group
justifies its own behavior—the upper middle class judges itself to be "moral," while the lower class calls itself
"natural." [4]

The upper middle class also places much more emphasis
on striving and achievement. The family, teachers, and
even at times the peer group apply pressure on the child
to study, seek good grades, strive for scholarships, and
attain a respectable business or professional position. If
the child does well, he gains approval, esteem, and other
rewards; if not, he receives disapproval and punishment.
No epithet is more humiliating than "stupid." Allison
Davis suggests that such pressure on the upper-middle-
class child makes him anxious to succeed and that this
anxiety itself then becomes an important motivating force.
He strives eagerly for the goals held up as desirable and
is concerned lest he fail. Since his anxiety impels him
towards behavior that is socially valued in the society at
large, Davis speaks of it as "adaptive" or "socialized"
anxiety.[5]

Accompanying anxiety of this kind is the development of a *deferred gratification pattern:* the child learns to postpone immediate gratifications for the rewards he might achieve in the future. If he works hard at his studies, saves money, and avoids serious sexual entanglements, he may more easily attain a position which accords him wealth, prestige, and influence. To be sure, the child who defers gratifications does have some compensations in the process, for he derives satisfactions from the progress he is making and the approval from his significant others.

Contrast this upper-middle-class picture of adaptive anxiety and deferred gratification with the situation of the lower-class child. Davis suggests that the latter is so concerned with problems of immediate living that ambition is a luxury:

> This terrible pressure for physical survival means that the child . . . usually does not learn the "ambition," the drive for high skills, and for educational achievement that the middle-class child learns in his family. . . . [These strong incentives and difficult goals] have been submerged in his family life by the daily battle for food, shelter, and for the preservation of the family. In this sense, ambition and the drive to attain the higher skills are a kind of luxury.[6]

Nor, since the rewards offered by the middle class are too distant to be meaningful, does the lower-class child learn and internalize a deferred gratification pattern. He is not stigmatized for failure in school and is not motivated to sacrifice for future gains.

> To the underprivileged adolescent, the words and goals of his teacher—those words and goals to which middle-class adolescents react with respect and hard striving—mean very little. For the words of the teacher are not connected with the *acts of training in his home,* with the actual rewards in school, or with actual steps in moving toward a career. . . . The underprivileged workers . . . can win the rewards of prestige and social acceptance in their slum groups without much education.[7]

The upper-middle- and lower-class child both learn where they fit into the class system and the expectations of their social level in the ordinary course of development. In various ways the significant others of the child define class positions. The designations are not as explicit as the English upper-class "N.O.C.D." ("not our class, dear"),[8] but, in one way or another, class designations are expressed. An upper-middle-class parent may speak of "leather-jacket hoodlums" or the "social elite" or suggest the propriety of a private room in the hospital for someone in his position. The lower-class person may refer to "the rich people," the union man who settled down, or the "ignorant bum."

Children also learn of class behavior and identification through their role-taking models. The child in the upper-middle-class family is not only told to be neat, careful of his language, and quiet in church; he actually observes such behavior in his immediate environment. His models also indicate their class level by deferring to high-ranking professional people and, in their turn, by expecting deference from domestic help and store clerks. Similarly, the child of the lower class learns through his role-taking models. He hears the language of the streets, sees his family share food with relatives, and observes the casual attitudes to property and relatively free sex behavior. Speaking of the non-postponement of gratifications, Davis describes one aspect of the model as follows:

> He gets strong biological enjoyment. He spends a great deal of his nights in sexual exploration. . . . Recreation, relaxation, and pure laziness from Friday night through Sunday night are extremely satisfying experiences. If such a weekend leaves the worker too exhausted to get on the job Monday or even Tuesday . . . it nevertheless is so organically rewarding that he will repeat the experience the following weekend, or certainly the following payday.[9]

The Middle Class and the Working Class. Between the middle and lower classes in the urban world is a large segment of skilled and semi-skilled laborers spoken of broadly as the "working-class" or "common-man" group. These men ordinarily have steady jobs, possibly a high school education, and reside in respectable areas. Many live in suburbs and own their own homes.

In many respects, the values of this group are similar to those of the upper middle class. Working-class parents too are likely to stress polite manners, good personal habits, and sexual restraints. In a recent study in Washington, D.C., Melvin L. Kohn reports that mothers of both groups share a common set of values for their 10- and 11-year-old children. Kohn writes:

There is considerable agreement among mothers of both social classes that happiness and such standards of conduct as honesty, consideration, obedience, dependability, manners and self-control are highly desirable for both boys and girls at this age.[10]

However, different degrees of importance and sometimes different meanings are given to the same values. Thus the working class gives greater weight to obedience, neatness, and cleanliness; and the middle class to self-control, curiosity, and happiness. Kohn suggests that the parents of each group accord high priority to those values which they consider are important for the child's future, but difficult to achieve. For the working class, "important but problematic" concerns center around qualities that insure respectability; for the middle class, respectability is taken for granted and the "important but problematic" matters relate to internalized standards of conduct:

The [middle-class] child is to act appropriately, not because his parents tell him to, but because he wants to. Not conformity to authority, but inner control; not because you're told to but because you take the other person into consideration.[11]

Other differences of course also exist between middle- and working-class groups: they often belong to different clubs, enjoy different recreations, vote differently, read different magazines, spend different proportions of their income on formal education, and have different aspirations for their children. The attitude of a bread salesman whose

son had an I.Q. score in the upper quintile may not be
typical, but it is not uncommon:

> No matter what I would like [my son] to do, it isn't my
> job to say so as he may not be qualified. I tried to tell him
> where he isn't going to be a doctor or lawyer or anything
> like that. I told him he should learn English and learn to
> meet people. Then he could go out and sell something
> worthwhile where a sale would amount to something for
> him.[12]

Many researchers have compared the early child-rearing
patterns of middle- and working-class groups. The results
of these studies are inconsistent, partly because the samples
are not always comparable and the research techniques
differ and partly because the patterns themselves have
changed. A recent summary report concludes that between
about 1930 and 1945, working-class mothers were uni-
formly more permissive and indulgent than the middle
class in child-rearing patterns; and that they more often
followed self-demand schedules, breastfed their babies,
and weaned and toilet-trained them at a later age. In
recent years, however, middle-class mothers, partly as a
result of the advice of child guidance specialists, have
become the more permissive in these areas and it is the
working class which is more severe.[13] Precisely what these
differences mean for socialization is not clear.

Some studies further report that techniques of control
differ between middle- and working-class groups. Working-
class parents are more likely to employ ridicule and
physical punishment, while middle-class adults depend
more directly on psychological ties between the child and
his parents. Instead of punishing physically, middle-class
parents express disappointment, offer symbolic rewards
and punishments, and appeal to the child's conscience. If
he does not cooperate, he may lose his parents' love or at
least disturb a mutually valued relationship.[14]

Kohn, in his Washington study, obtains somewhat
different results.[15] Middle-class parents, he reports, resort
to physical punishment about as frequently as do working-

class parents. However, they do so under different circumstances; some actions, intolerable to working-class parents, are not punished by their middle-class opposites and *vice versa*. Since working-class parents, Kohn argues, seek to inculcate qualities that insure respectability, desirable behavior consists essentially of not violating proscriptions. Therefore they tend to respond in terms of the immediate consequences of the child's actions and punish physically, for example, for fighting with siblings or for relatively wild play.

Since the middle-class parent, on the contrary, values the development of internalized standards of conduct, desirable behavior consists essentially of acting according to the dictates of one's own principles. The middle-class parent then is more likely to respond in terms of his interpretation of the child's intention. Therefore, relatively fewer middle-class parents physically punish their sons for wild play since this is but a childish form of emotional expression, unpleasant but bearable. An outburst of temper, however, *is* physically punished, for it signals serious difficulty in the child's attempt at self-mastery and distresses the parent who has tried to inculcate the virtue of self-control. These findings and interpretations are highly suggestive, to be sure, but they are not conclusive, especially in view of the fact that the investigations were made in a highly mobile society.

Mobility. Many factors promote upward social mobility in the United States, including an expanding economy, the increasing proportion of highly trained people, and differential birth rates. Sometimes this mobility has involved entire groups, for example, Negroes, Russian Jews, and skilled labor have moved up the social ladder relative to other groups. Of course, mobility also applies to individuals: the son of a janitor becomes an accountant or the daughter of a railway clerk marries an engineer.[16] The proportion of downwardly mobile individuals—the "skidders"—is not as great, although it is substantial.[17]

The child in the upwardly mobile family, or the child

who becomes mobile himself, faces distinctive problems of socialization. The child of the lower class, for example, may not, in the ordinary course of his family experiences, learn an upper-middle-class style of life or develop upper-middle-class aspirations. If he is to be mobile, he requires such other sources of knowledge and influence as teachers, relatives of higher social status, or the mass media.

Learning the ways of the group to which he aspires is one problem for the mobile person; developing the psychologically appropriate self-image and group identification is another. As we have observed, a change of status involves a change of self-image. Sometimes status changes are clearly defined—a civilian becomes a soldier, a girl becomes a student nurse, a boy becomes president of a club. In such cases, the person may change his behavior greatly, but the expectations are unambiguous and the transition may not involve serious problems.

Moving up into a new social class introduces different problems, and whether or not the transition occurs smoothly is influenced by numerous contingent factors. Where class lines have been relatively sharp as in England (until recently, at least) or where the problems of social class are compounded by problems of ethnic or racial affiliation, the mobile person may feel ill at ease or the higher status group may not accept him. Even his original class group might view him askance. Speaking of the "scholarship boy" in England, Richard Hoggart writes:

> He cannot face squarely his own working class. . . . If he tries to be "pally" with working-class people, to show that he is one of them, they "smell it a mile off." They are less at ease with him than with some in other classes.[18]

Developing an appropriate self-image is thereby made all the more difficult. By comparison, in our society, the problem of a higher class identification for the mobile person is ordinarily tempered. To be sure, he adopts certain new behavior patterns and forms new associations; however, these changes are made easier for him by the corresponding situation of many acquaintances, the blurred class lines, the comparatively vaguely defined social class expectations, and the somewhat contrary values of individual autonomy and egalitarianism, which permit certain nonconforming behavior.

Mobility, we have suggested, has not occurred equally for all groups in the society. Ethnic groups especially vary in the amount of upward mobility and the emphasis their members place on mobility in socialization patterns and processes. Although we cannot in a few pages do justice to a problem so broad and complicated, we discuss certain aspects of the relationship between ethnic groups and mobility in the following section.[19]

Ethnic Groups

The population of North America derives from immigrants from many countries. Those whose families came several generations ago from northern Europe are now ordinarily thought of as native Americans, those whose families came more recently from such countries as Greece, Poland, Hungary, and Mexico are more often considered ethnic minorities.

The mass immigration of relatively uneducated southern and eastern Europeans to the United States was halted by legislation passed in the early 1920s, and relatively few European immigrants of similar backgrounds have come since. In recent years, however, Mexicans and especially Puerto Ricans have arrived in large numbers. The Puerto Ricans, who are American citizens, number over 750,000 in the United States, of whom three quarters live in New York City. Currently, then, for Puerto Ricans and many Mexicans, it is the first and second generations who are being socialized into American life; for the older immigrant groups, it is generally the third generation and beyond.

The adaptation of any ethnic group to American culture depends on such contingent factors as the group's degree of cohesion; its particular skills and educational level; its degree of deviance from American culture; popular images

of its native country and people, and the economic, political, and social conditions prevailing in the United States at the time of its arrival. Thus there are many variations between and within ethnic groups, but the process of socialization for immigrants and their descendants nevertheless presents certain characteristic patterns.

Various studies indicate that minority-group children are aware of their distinct statuses by the time they are six or seven years old and often before that, although they are too young to understand abstract aspects of status differe..tiations.[20] Compared with other children, they "show earlier and greater differentiation of their own group as well as more personal involvement in the group identification." [21]

The child learns his ethnic status in the normal course of deveiopment. His significant others serve as models for behavior and feelings associated with ethnic status, and, often in such questions as "Why am I Polish?" or "Why can't I have a Christmas tree?" he expresses awareness of differences between himself and others.

An ethnic status is only one of several statuses that a child learns, and, depending on the situation, it becomes of greater or lesser importance in his thought and behavior. Does he feel more comfortable with members of his own group than with others? Does he adopt easily or with difficulty, if at all, the restrictions and cautions which his status seems to call for? Does he acknowledge the right of the in-group to exert pressure on him? Does he accept prejudices of the larger society and disparage his own group? Does he follow his peers or his parents if they disagree about status group expectations? These are just a few of the questions relevant to ethnic status. The general process of development for the child of an ethnic minority group is no different from normal processes of socialization, but certain problems of status identification are accentuated.

In the following sections, we discuss socialization in the second generation and in the third, recognizing of course that the lines between generations are necessarily blurred.

Socialization in the Second Generation. The child of the immigrant learns two cultures and two identities, those of his ethnic group and those of the United States. His ethnic culture and identity are learned through hearing stories of group experiences, idealizing group heroes, observing and sympathizing with family members in their behavior with fellow ethnics and outsiders, and generally through participating in the group's way of life. He learns the culture, not in its "pure" form but as modified and practiced in the new country. Speaking of the Puerto Ricans, Elena Padilla writes:

> The culture of Puerto Ricans in New York cannot be characterized as "Puerto Rican," for it is not the same as that of Puerto Ricans in Puerto Rico. . . . Even the Spanish language spoken in New York differs from that of Puerto Rico. . . . Many of these [words and phrases] are derived from English and assimilated into the Spanish the migrants brought with them.[22]

Outside of his immediate family and ethnic group, the child experiences the new American society and culture with their different customs, loyalties, and prejudices. Those aspects of the new world that are derived from advertisements, movies, headlines, and department store displays are likely to be characteristic of the country as a whole in contrast with those that are derived from a limited local setting. Immigrants who live in the lowest-rent neighborhoods often learn about the United States from a distinctly "slum point of view."

Perhaps the most important agency of socialization teaching the broader American culture is the school. Anthropologist Toshio Yatsushiro, writing of the second generation Japanese on the West Coast, says:

> More than any other single force, the American school molded the character of the Nisei. . . . They responded eagerly to the relatively free and permissive school atmosphere which was in direct contrast to the rigid family life they led. They were able to interact rather freely with the members of the majority group, and in doing so assimilated

. . . traits of the majority culture. Among other things, they were quick to pick up slang and cursing.[23]

That misunderstandings, frustrations, and conflicts develop between parents and children in such cases is not surprising. The parents, with their traditional set of values, are often dismayed at the behavior and attitudes of their children, and the latter, in turn, resent the ideas of their parents. The comment of a Mexican-American girl is not atypical:

> My mother and dad got too many old-fashioned ideas. She's from another country. I'm from America, and I'm not like her. With Mexican girls they want you to sit like *moscas muertas,* dead flies, like that. If you tell them what the teachers say, they say the teachers don't know. . . . I remember when me and my sister told my mother we wanted to dress neat and American they beat us and said no.[24]

In such cases, it is generally the immigrant parents, unable to draw on a culture and social system to support their position, who must try to make the major adaptations.

The child of the ethnic minority group has two statuses, he is both Mexican, Japanese, or Italian, say, and American. The images and feelings which the two groups have of themselves and each other may not correspond. A child, as a Greek, may be proud of his national heritage and religion; as an American, he may be aware of his foreign-sounding name and his parents' strong accent. Because of his ethnic origin, many of his peers may reject him, or, even if they don't, he still fears that they may do so.

For the child, this double identity may—although, of course, it need not—lead to problems of "marginality." The child lives on the margins of two cultures and has loyalties to both, but is completely a member of neither. Each group membership offers satisfactions, but each also offers anxieties. A comment by a second-generation Italian illustrates the difficulty of developing a consistent and integrated self-image:

As an Italian-American, I occasionally use my hands to stress my points. . . . The Italians are great gesturers, so I probably inherited it; but not to that degree, because I have educated myself to restrain it. When I let my hair down, I resort to gesturing in a fine form. But when I realize what I'm doing, I guard against it.[25]

But whatever the problems, the members of the second generation do learn the basic elements of American culture and, as socializing agents for the third generation, are undoubtedly "American."

Socialization in the Third Generation. Most members of the third generation readily assimilate the major elements of American culture and their class positions within it. That they no longer speak the language of the old country or follow traditional customs does not bother them. Nevertheless, the values of the past are not completely lost; they persist particularly in their orientation towards achievement and their ethnic or religious identification.

In the previous section, we mentioned the relationship between ethnic group and social class. In earlier generations, new immigrants, often having come from rural or "peasant" areas and without specialized training, began at the lowest socio-economic rungs in the society and "pushed up" those who had arrived before them. Robin Williams writes:

So long as each year brought large numbers of new immigrants, a shifting and flexible hierarchy could develop in which each new group entered at the bottom of the "pecking order" only to move up later to a position of dominance over newer groups.[26]

For the grandchildren of immigrants, this "progression in status" no longer holds, for different ethnic groups have advanced at different rates. Some, by virtue of their traditions and socialization patterns, have absorbed more easily than others American values of mobility and achievement. For example, in comparing Jews and Italians in New

Haven, Fred L. Strodtbeck reports that "Jews consistently have higher occupational status than the population at large, while, in contrast, Italians are consistently lower." [27]

The differences in achievement orientation are well brought out in Bernard Rosen's recent study in four Northeastern states of six racial and ethnic groups— French Canadians, Greeks, Southern Italians, East European Jews, Negroes, and native-born white Protestants.[28] Four hundred twenty-seven pairs of mothers and sons, the latter generally third generation or more, were interviewed. Rosen compares these groups in achievement motivations, relevant value orientations, and aspiration levels, which, together, make up an "achievement syndrome." For each component of the syndrome, the white Protestants, Jews, and Greeks ranked higher than the French Canadians and Italians. The former groups more often imposed standards of excellence, set high goals, and expected self-reliant behavior from their children; more often upheld values which implement achievement-motivated behavior, such as individual responsibility, future planning, and active striving for goals, and had higher educational and vocational aspirations. For example, in reply to a question on the "floor" of vocational aspirations, 48 per cent of the Italian and 52 per cent of the French Canadian mothers would be satisfied to have their sons become department store salesmen, compared with 12 per cent of the Jewish, 22 per cent of the white Protestant, and 29 per cent of the Greek mothers.

Historical and ethnographic data indicate that differences between these groups existed before their arrival in the United States.[29] The Jews and Greeks—as well as the Protestants, who are heir to the Puritan ethic—have traditionally stressed self-reliance, education, concern with the future, success strivings, and the possibility of rationally mastering the world. The southern Italians and French Canadians, generally coming from agrarian societies in which the individual has less control of his life situation, have traditionally been less oriented towards achievement. In their socialization practices, the latter groups, in contrast to the former, did not urge their children to set their sights high or exhort them to strive for achievement.

Of course, these differences between ethnic groups represent only tendencies. Class position is another important variable. In all ethnic groups, middle-class parents stress achievement and success more strongly than do working-class adults. Moreover, with a generally increasing standard of living and with the birth of fourth and fifth generations, there is no assurance that the distinctions of the present will continue into the future.

For the child of the third generation, the assimilation of American culture has not meant group absorption. In fact, recently, some ethnic minorities—especially Jews—have consciously stressed ethnic identification. The intellectual defense of this emphasis derives in part from the writings of the late Kurt Lewin, who affirmed the dangers among minority group members of "self-hatred." In every underprivileged group, Lewin claimed, there seems to exist:

> . . . a tendency to accept the values of the more privileged group. . . . The member of the underprivileged group therefore becomes excessively sensitive to everything within his own group that does not conform to those values because it makes him feel that he belongs to a group whose standards are lower.[30]

He may, as a consequence, feel contempt for himself and his own group. To avoid this danger, Lewin suggests that a minority group should affirm its identity and build up "a clear and positive feeling of belongingness." In this way, within the context of modern American life, Jewish groups, especially in the middle class, are emphasizing Jewish holidays and religious practices. The child is taught that he is American, but within the American system, he belongs to a distinctly Jewish ethnic-religious community.[31]

The tendency for Jewish groups to minimize internal divisions in the interest of a general Jewish identification applies, as well, some observers suggest, to Catholics and Protestants.[32] Excluding non-white groups, they speak of a "triple" religious melting pot in which children learn that they are, religiously, Protestant, Catholic, or Jewish, and that the particular national or ethnic origin is of lesser importance. With more evidence, we shall know whether or not this is a definite trend. But, in any case, we recognize that many third-generation immigrants, although undoubtedly "American," affirm more readily than their parents their ethnic and religious identification.

Suburbia

Sociologists traditionally have distinguished between the rural and the urban way of life. In the rural setting, social relationships are said to be more personal and "primary." Everyone knows everyone else and social control is maintained through gossip, reputation, and other informal means. In the event of an individual crisis, relatives and neighbors rally round to give assistance. Sex and generation statuses are clearly differentiated, with little confusion about the duties and rights of father, mother, son, daughter, and grandparents. In the idealized picture of rural life there is little variation between the life of one generation and the next, so boys and girls, when quite young, can be prepared for the roles they will carry out as adults.

In contrast, life in the metropolitan city is characterized by mobility and rapid social change, secondary and impersonal relationships predominate, neighbors may not know each other. For the child, competitive pressure is greater, the customs and limits of acceptable behavior are less clearly defined, and the expectations for the future are more obscure.

This contrast means that one important problem of socialization is the adjustment of the country-born child who moves to the city. This problem is currently very important for urban migrants in underdeveloped countries, but in North America and most of the Western world it is rapidly diminishing. A sweeping cultural urbanization of most rural and small-town life has all but eliminated major cultural differences between rural and urban. In present-day America, both farm and city residents see the same

TV shows, read the same advertisements, use the same electrical appliances, belong to similar branches of national organizations, obey the same government regulations, and follow similar fashions.[33]

In North America, in recent years, the most important trend in population redistribution has been the growth of the suburb. With superhighways, fast commuter train service, and the decentralization of both industry and retail trade, millions of families have moved to the outskirts of cities, and now over one fourth of the American population is suburban. Suburbs are of many types: residential and industrial, well-to-do and working-class,[34] with and without commercial centers, newly built and mass-produced or long-established with traditions and socially important families. Here we stress the most prominent of recent suburban developments, the middle-class residential suburb.

Life in the Suburb. The middle-class suburb is family-centered, with few single adults and few old people. The proportion of families with small children is high, many of them having three or more children. One sociologist hypothesizes that "the move to the suburb expresses an attempt to find a location in which to conduct family life which is more suitable than that offered by central cities," [35] and, as part of his evidence, cites a survey of two Chicago suburbs in which 80 per cent of the respondents said that they had moved to obtain better conditions for their children. They sought more space, "the outdoors," less traffic, better schools, and "nice children to play with." The popular writer, A. C. Spectorsky, speaking of the "exurb," which lies just beyond the ordinary suburb, similarly writes:

> A couple may have had all sorts of bemused reasons for moving so far from the city, but the wife had one compelling one: her children are out of the city in the country, away from expensive private schools or inferior public schools, with plenty of children just like themselves for companionship.[36]

The middle-class suburb is relatively homogeneous —without slums or mansions, with few foreign or strange accents, and marked by a limited range of incomes. Neighbors are of similar ages and in about the same stage of the family cycle. With such homogeneity, community cleavages are less likely to develop about schools, taxes, zoning regulations, and other common concerns. The similar occupational and leisure interests of the residents also encourage neighborhood activities and informal interaction.[37]

Neighborliness, in fact, is especially outstanding in reports of suburban life. Authors speak of the friendly spirit, free and easy visiting patterns, coffee klatsches, local newspaper gossip, "welcome wagons" for newcomers, and the sharing of tools, advice, and energies. Often, residents participate in a communal life of baby-sitting services, bridge clubs, hobby groups, car pools, and cooperative nurseries. Although the following statement of an Illinois housewife is extreme, it suggests a tendency:

> At the beginning we were maybe too neighborly—your friends knew more about your private life than you did yourself! It's not quite that active now. But it's still real friendly—even our dogs and cats are friendly with one another! The street behind us is nowhere near as friendly. They knock on doors over there.[38]

Suburban residents participate widely in local activities, often withdrawing from previous urban associations. For men, and some women, civic committees are important. In one Eastern suburb, the Mayor and City Council are assisted by voluntary citizens' committees on safety, city planning, public relations, civil defense, finance, parks and playgrounds, civic library, industrial development, architecture, engineering, and public welfare. For women with school-age children, perhaps no organization is more significant than the Parent-Teachers Association. One study describes the PTA as "the most important voluntary association" in the community.[39]

Two counter trends are often noted in middle-class suburbs—one towards tolerance, the other towards conformity. Tolerance is particularly evident in religious practices. Where Protestants, Catholics, and Jews live together, they may "lean over backwards" to cooperate in community affairs. And Protestant groups in suburbs have formed as many as 1,700 non-denominational community churches. One such church in Illinois is described as a "believe-as-you-like, worship-as-you-please fellowship of searchers." The team of ministers, all equal in authority, includes a Baptist, Methodist, and Congregationalist.[40]

Conformity is evident in the stigma of being an "isolate" and in the pressure to be friendly and to participate in local activities. Neighbors, too, notoriously compare each other's lawns, Christmas displays, cars, furniture, and children. To be ostentatious in displaying one's possessions or achievements is as reprehensible as not conforming. One must keep "down" as well as "up" with the Joneses. It is this pressure to conform which so many writers deplore:

> Writers point to the uniformity of the ranch style, the ever-present television antennae, the lamp in the picture-window. Observers have been struck by a kind of massification of men. . . . [One author] discusses the . . . excessive dependency of development dwellers on each other and on experts, coupled with monotony both in exterior trim and internalized affects.[41]

Socialization in the Suburb. What does this type of middle-class suburban life mean for socialization? Above all else, it means a protective setting.[42] With a homogeneous population, the child, both in neighborhood and school, meets children very much like himself. Moreover, since the community is often "self-contained" in its own local services and recreational facilities, the child, except for special occasions, does not cross community boundaries. Therefore he not only experiences few hardships, he has little opportunity to become directly familiar with ways of life which differ greatly from his own.

The protective setting is supplemented by the structuring of the child's time. He spends several hours a week doing homework, he helps in household activities, takes music or dancing lessons, and participates in school organizations, directed sports, and church and "Y" activities. His parents generally know what he is doing and with whom. A mother in a Montreal suburb, quite characteristically, said of her adolescent son:

> I make it a point of knowing what he is doing. If he can't be home one afternoon when he's expected, he'll leave a note telling me what he's up to. I like to know where he is. If, for any reason, he's going to be late, he calls and lets us know.[43]

And more than just keeping close watch, the parents in this community guide and direct many of the child's activities. They discuss his school courses, welcome his guests into their homes, and assist in his social gatherings. They decide, in collusion with other parents, the size of allowances and the number of dates permitted each week. In one instance, when a boy and girl began "going steady," their parents conferred—as, no doubt, many parents do— to discuss whether or not the relationship should be encouraged.

Nor do reports of middle-class suburban life suggest that children overtly resist this protective environment. They generally accept the parents' prerogative of supervising their lives, willingly report details of their activities (except sexual behavior), and express little desire to participate in activities outside the local community.

Of particular significance in socialization are the models which parents and other adults present to the child. To a great degree, as we have observed, the lives of the parents are circumscribed within the limits of the community. Sons may not, as in rural areas, see their fathers work at their occupations, but they do see them in many other roles. Furthermore, parents and children often do things together—they visit relatives, entertain guests, and attend the school's dramatic and athletic events. Do-it-yourself activities often become family affairs. Ernest R. Mowrer, writing of a Chicago suburb, says:

When the suburban husband turns indoors, he is often joined by his wife and together they become interior craftsmen, painting walls and ceilings, hanging paper, and refinishing furniture.[44]

Children too may have a part. An adolescent boy in a Montreal suburb reports:

On Saturday morning, I help my father around the house. We've been building a recreation room downstairs. We cemented the walls, fixed up a place for cold storage, and now we've just started on the furnace room. We're going to do the garage next and we're building a patio too. We both get a kick out of it.[45]

Suburban parental-role models are flexible and often tend towards the egalitarian type. The wife may perform characteristically masculine jobs such as shoveling snow from walks, caring for the yard and garden, and driving other members of the family to their destinations. And the husband, besides being a general handyman, may become a "mother's helper," assisting with household tasks and feeding and diapering the infants.[46]

Our generalizations about suburbia must be viewed with caution. As yet, we have few scientific studies of suburban life, and many reports are little more than superficial impressions. Nor, often, can we distinguish suburban trends from trends in American life as a whole. Furthermore, the changes in recent years have been so rapid that a suburb today may be very different from the same suburb five years ago. That patterns different from the one described may develop is indicated in a recent portrait of Levittown, Long Island, a suburb which tends to fuse middle- and working-class groups. For example, on the subject of neighborliness:

Friendship patterns on any street in Levittown are likely to be deliberate and depend more upon occupational and intellectual interests than on neighborhood arrangements. Family-visiting of neighbors is rare when compared to the volume of entertainment that exists on other bases.[47]

Or, on "community spirit," the same author remarks that three out of four residents do seem to feel a sense of community, but many pressures—for example, a transient population, diversity of occupation and education, variation in geographic, ethnic, and religious background, and especially a number of potentially divisive problems—discourage the further development of fellowship bonds.[48]

While we cannot speak with assurance about the pattern of socialization for the suburban child, there is little doubt about the increasing signficance of this setting for both middle- and working-class children. This is an important area for further study.

6 CONCLUSION: SOCIALIZATION IN LATER LIFE

Socialization continues throughout life. A freshman is socialized into the patterns of a college, an immigrant into the life of a new country, a recruit into the army, a new resident into a suburb, a medical student into the profession, a new patient into a hospital ward, and a bride into a life of marriage. But adult socialization differs from that of the child in that the adult has already developed a more or less established character structure and his significant others have more limited involvements. The basic elements of the adult socialization process, however, are similar to that of the child. The socializing agents teach, serve as models, and invite participation. Through their ability to offer gratifications and deprivations, they induce cooperation and learning and prevent disrupting deviance. Individuals being socialized, on their part, through observation, participation, and role-taking, learn and internalize new expectations and develop new self-conceptions.

From the perspective of any ongoing social grouping— be it an association, occupation, class, ethnic group, or society as a whole—its persistence, in its existing form, depends on socialization, on the learning by new recruits and participants of both necessary skills and appropriate attitudes and sentiments. The infantry recruit should learn not only the basic skills of fighting, he should also know the traditions and slang of his unit, feel solidarity with his group, and believe that commands should come through a military hierarchy. The insurance agent learns not only the technicalities of selling and writing policies, he also learns a professional self-conception and the arguments to justify pressure techniques. Unless a new member of a group is adequately socialized into appropriate skills, thoughts, and feelings, he cannot effectively carry out his role, including his part in the socialization of a new "generation."

Socialization into a new grouping may occur informally in the routines of interaction. The patterns of a suburb, for example, with its neighborhood shopping, friendship relations, and lawn decorations are not formally taught; rather, a new resident learns these through participation in suburban life. Socialization into some social worlds, however, especially those that require technical skills, involves a combination of formal and informal techniques. In learning to be a physician, the medical student quite formally learns anatomy, diagnosis, prescription writing, and other specific skills. In his formal training he is also taught certain ideals and norms such as medical ethics and appropriate relationships between professional workers in the hospital. At the same time, much of his socialization is informal. Through stories, general observation, and the way doctors, students, patients, nurses, and others behave toward him, he learns that certain old-time nurses have considerable degrees of knowledge and power, that certain physicians prominent in the community have questionable reputations in the profession, that some aspects of medical ethics may be evaded and others may not. As a by-product of his training, he may also develop a professional conscience and come to feel a hatred of medical charlatans and a solidarity with fellow physicians. This informal socialization continues in the course of his career. In seeking sponsorship for a hospital appointment he may learn how to sidestep local rivalries; through participation in a medical association, he may learn the sanctions applied to non-conforming colleagues; through visits by drug company representatives, he may learn "short-cut" methods of keeping up with medical research.[1]

Socialization, in all these instances, involves a changing image of oneself. For the adult—whether soldier, business executive, suburban resident, or social worker—this changing self-conception has its beginnings in his aspirations and training, for he sees himself in terms of the future.[2] The self-image becomes further elaborated and established when the actual status is attained. So the new policeman views himself as a city employee, as deserving of respect and obedience, and perhaps as misunderstood by a goodly portion of the public. The new schoolteacher sees himself as having a worthy profession, a responsibility to his pupils, and a position superior in prestige—but not in income—to the factory worker. This new self-image is formed in part by training, formal and informal, in part by the expectations and behavior of others, and in part by reinforcement by fellow workers.

Adopting a group's perspective in socialization means a confinement as well as a focus of thought. The business executive, for example, may come to think of all labor unions as obstructionist, and the psychiatrist may seek unconscious motives in explaining a very large part of behavior. Thus specific group perspectives may mean an inability—or, using Veblen's phrase, a "trained incapacity" [3] —to see situations from other perspectives.

For an adult, socialization into a new system may occur readily and easily or it may introduce distinctive problems. The new army recruit may be unwilling or unable to accept a situation of strict authority; the college freshman may be unwilling or unable to participate in college and student activities. In such instances, assuming that the recruit learns and carries through enough of the army expectations to avoid being imprisoned or discharged, and the student sufficiently follows the rules and expectations of the college to avoid expulsion, we may speak of *partial socialization.* From the perspective of the ongoing group, such persons carry out their roles to only a limited degree.

Sometimes a person's formal training and image of his prospective position are so different from his subsequent experiences that he suffers "reality shock." A graduate of a secretarial school, for example, may look forward to a pleasant and interesting job with a company executive and instead do only routine typing and filing. A librarian may look forward to a position of public service and prestige and instead find only a disrespecting public interested in "escape" reading.

The "shock" for workers in bureaucratic organizations probably comes less from the formal than the informal structure. The informal "other face" of a bureaucracy, an inevitable development in formal organizations, has its own sanctions, norms, and system of communication. The grapevine may disclose "shameful" bits of information about department personnel, and the employees may undermine company goals and circumvent official procedures. A person with an important formal status, if considered an "apple-polisher" by his fellow workers, may be rejected socially; another, with a less important formal position, may be the group's "natural leader." For the employee being socialized, such aspects of the informal system, not trained for and unanticipated, may constitute the "reality shock." [4]

Socialization occurs all through life. In a society as rapidly changing as our own, there are always new developments and relationships that must be learned. Children teach their parents popular songs, slang, and the current patterns of their peer groups.[5] Inventions such as television lead to changing recreation patterns and contacts with new technicians. Industrial and business expansion necessitates adaptations to new policies and new personnel. Developments in international politics may lead to an influx of immigrants and "fashionable" opinions about political leaders. In these and many other areas, socialization is a process that never ceases.

NOTES AND REFERENCES

CHAPTER 2 *Preconditions for Socialization*

1. The following works illustrate sociological perspectives in detail: Kingsley Davis, *Human Society,* New York: Macmillan, 1948; R. M. MacIver and C. H. Page, *Society: An Introductory Analysis,* New York: Rinehart, 1949; and Ely Chinoy, *Sociological Perspective: Basic Concepts and Their Application,* New York: Random House, 1954.
2. Charles H. Cooley, *Human Nature and the Social Order,* Boston: Scribner, 1902.
3. Charles H. Cooley, *Social Organization,* New York: Scribner, 1912, Chap. III.
4. Kingsley Davis, "Final Note on a Case of Extreme Isolation," *American Journal of Sociology,* Vol. LII (1947), pp. 432-437.
5. René A. Spitz, "Hospitalism," *The Psychoanalytic Study of the Child,* Vol. I (1945), pp. 53-72; and "Hospitalism: A Follow-up Report," *ibid.,* Vol. II (1946), pp. 113-117.
6. J. A. L. Singh and Robert M. Zingg, *Wolf Children and Feral Man,* New York: Harper, 1939.
7. Bruno Bettelheim, "Feral Children and Autistic Children," *American Journal of Sociology,* Vol. LXIV (1959), pp. 455-467.
8. See, for example, John Bowlby, *Child Care and the Growth of Love,* London: Penguin, 1953; Theodore R. Sarbin and Donal S. Jones, "Intrapersonal Factors in Delinquency: A Preliminary Report," *Nervous Child,* Vol. 11 (1955), pp. 23-27.

CHAPTER 3 *The Process of Socialization*

1. See Neal Gross, W. S. Mason and A. W. McEachern, *Explorations in Role Analysis: Studies of the School Superintendency Role*, New York: Wiley, 1958. In Part 1, the authors discuss varied uses of "role," giving particular emphasis to the problem of role consensus.

2. Talcott Parsons, *The Social System*, Glencoe, Ill.: The Free Press, 1951, Chap. II, and Hans Gerth and C. Wright Mills, *Character and Social Structure*, New York: Harcourt, Brace, 1953, pp. 10-15.

3. For an excellent analysis of the relationship between individual development and certain social variables with a focus on personality organization, see David P. Ausubel, "The Relationship between Social Variables and Ego Development and Functioning," in M. Sherif and M. O. Wilson, eds., *Emerging Problems in Social Psychology*, Norman, Oklahoma: Institute of Group Relations, University of Oklahoma, 1957, pp. 55-96.

4. Jean Piaget, *Language and Thought of the Child*, London: Routledge and Kegan Paul, 1932.

5. Jean Piaget, *Moral Judgment of the Child*, Glencoe, Ill.: The Free Press, 1948.

6. Margaret Mead in *Discussions on Child Development*, eds. J. M. Tanner and B. Inhelder, London: Tavistock, 1958, pp. 88-89.

7. Ruth Benedict, "Continuities and Discontinuities in Cultural Conditioning," *Psychiatry*, Vol. 2 (1938), pp. 161-167.

8. Robert F. Bales and P. E. Slater, "Role Differentiation in Small Decision-Making Groups," in Talcott Parsons and Robert F. Bales, *Family, Socialization and Interaction Process*, Glencoe, Ill.: The Free Press, 1955, p. 259.

9. Some current guides to parents advise them to affirm their love for the child at the same time as they punish him. It is, however, no simple matter for the child—or the parent—to distinguish the sanctions for a specific action and sanctions of a more general nature. Parsons, for purposes of analysis, in fact, distinguishes four types of sanctions: (1) *acceptance* or love for the child as a member of the family; (2) *esteem* for the child's general level of development; (3) *approval* for a child's specific

performance, and (4) *response,* for example, affection, following some specific behavior of the child. Response and approval are more directly related to socialization goals although, as clinical therapists have shown, their effectiveness depends in great part on acceptance and esteem. Talcott Parsons and Robert F. Bales, *op. cit.,* pp. 77ff. Also see Talcott Parsons, *The Social System,* pp. 219ff., for a discussion of the relationship between the affectively neutral rewards of "conditional love" and conditions which encourage identification and "growing up."

10. As Orville G. Brim points out, the prescription for a role often includes three elements: motivation, overt behavior, and effects. Parents, for example, should love their children, see that they are adequately clothed, and train them to be honest. Neither parents nor researchers generally make these distinctions, but theoretically they are separate and distinct. "The Parent-Child Relation as a Social System: I. Parent and Child Roles," *Child Development,* Vol. 28 (1957), pp. 343-364.

11. George H. Mead, *Mind, Self and Society,* Chicago: The University of Chicago Press, 1934, pp. 68ff.

12. For an insightful analysis of social relationships in terms of a theatrical perspective, with its "front" and "backstage" behavior, see Erving Goffman, *Presentation of Self in Everyday Life,* Edinburgh: University of Edinburgh Social Research Centre, 1957.

13. Anna Freud and Sophie Dann, "An Experiment in Group Upbringing," *The Psychoanalytic Study of the Child,* Vol. VI (1951), pp. 127-168. Cited in W. E. Martin and C. B. Stendler, *Readings in Child Development,* New York: Harcourt, Brace, 1954, p. 406.

14. For a discussion of gestures as a means of communication and index of cultural change among Italians and Jews in New York, see David Efron, *Gesture and Environment,* New York: King's Crown Press, 1941.

15. Edward Sapir, "Language," *Encyclopaedia of the Social Sciences,* New York: Macmillan, 1933, Vol. 9, p. 160.

16. See, for example, Robert K. Merton and Alice Kitt, "Contributions to the Theory of Reference Group Behavior," in Robert K. Merton and Paul F. Lazarsfeld (eds.), *Studies in the Scope and Method of "The American Soldier,"* Glencoe, Ill.: The Free Press, 1950, pp. 42-53; and Tamotsu Shibutani, "Reference Groups as Perspec-

tives," *American Journal of Sociology*, Vol. LX (1955), pp. 562-569.

17. George H. Mead, *op. cit.*, Part III.

18. *Ibid.*, pp. 150ff.

19. Talcott Parsons and Robert F. Bales, *op. cit.*, pp. 78-79.

20. C H. Cooley, *Human Nature and the Social Order, op. cit.*

21. Perhaps Freud gives the clearest exposition of his ideas in Sigmund Freud, *A General Introduction to Psychoanalysis*, New York: Garden City Publishing Co., 1935; and *An Outline of Psychoanalysis*, London: The Hogarth Press, 1949.

22. Irene M. Josselyn, *The Happy Child*, New York: Random House, 1955, p. 37.

23. Dorothy Burlingham and Anna Freud, *Young Children in War-Time*, London: George Allen & Unwin, 1942, p. 70.

24. Dorothy W. Baruch, *One Little Boy*, New York: Julian Press, 1952, p. 239.

25. *Ibid.*, pp. 237-238.

26. Sigmund Freud, *An Outline of Psychoanalysis*, p. 77.

27. Robert K. Merton, "The Self-Fulfilling Prophecy," *Antioch Review*, Vol. 8 (1948), pp. 193-210.

28. John B. Watson and Rosalie Raynor, "Conditioned Emotional Reactions," *Journal of Experimental Psychology*, Vol. 3 (1920), pp. 1-14.

29. Neal E. Miller and John Dollard, *Social Learning and Imitation*, New Haven: Yale University Press, 1941.

30. Psychoanalytic propositions that have been subjected to empirical tests have generally not been corroborated. See H. Orlansky, "Infant Care and Personality," *Psychological Bulletin*, Vol. 46 (1949), pp. 1-48; W. H. Sewell, "Infant Training and the Personality of the Child," *American Journal of Sociology*, Vol. LVIII (1953), pp. 150-159; and J. W. M. Whiting and I. L. Child, *Child Training and Personality*, New Haven: Yale University Press, 1953. Thus psychoanalysis, to date, remains essentially a clinical, and not empirical, approach.

CHAPTER 4 *Agencies of Socialization*

1. S. E. Morison, *The Puritan Pronaos*, New York: New York University Press, 1936, p. 10.

2. J. B. Watson, *Behaviorism,* New York: Norton, 1930, p. 104.

3. Jean Evans, *Three Men,* New York: Knopf, 1950, p. 11.

4. William A. Kephart, "A Quantitative Analysis of Intra-group Relationships," *American Journal of Sociology,* Vol. LV (1950), pp. 544-549. Also see James H. S. Bossard and Eleanor S. Boll, *The Large Family System,* Philadelphia: University of Pennsylvania Press, 1956; and Arnold W. Green, "The Middle Class Male Child and Neurosis," *American Sociological Review,* Vol. 11 (1946), pp. 31-41.

5. There is no consensus on the precise importance of early family experiences. Some authors affirm that early child rearing practices are the main determinant of a "basic personality structure," which in turn is the key factor in determining almost all beliefs and attitudes. See Abram Kardiner, *Psychological Frontiers of Society,* New York: Columbia University Press, 1939.

6. Harry Stack Sullivan, *Conceptions of Modern Psychiatry,* Washington: The William Alanson White Foundation, 1947.

7. See Erving Goffman, *op. cit.*

8. Claudia Lewis, *Children of the Cumberland,* New York: Columbia University Press, 1946, p. 88.

9. The tendency to forego immediate satisfactions for some future gain has been called the "deferred gratification pattern." For a brief review of the use of the concept, see Louis Schneider and Sverre Lysgaard, "The Deferred Gratification Pattern," *American Sociological Review,* Vol. 18 (1953), pp. 142-144. Also see Chapter 5, pp. 80-82.

10. Herman R. Lantz, *People of Coal Town,* New York: Columbia University Press, 1958, p. 260.

11. Robert Bierstedt, *The Social Order,* New York: McGraw-Hill Book Co., 1957, pp. 315-316.

12. On the basis of an extensive study of 41 boys, ages 8 and 11, Ruth E. Hartley suggestively analyzes the sources of tension and anxiety in the adoption of the male sex role. "Sex-Role Pressures and the Socialization of the Male Child," *Psychological Reports,* Vol. 5 (1959), pp. 457-468.

13. For an illustration of how some college girls experience this ambiguity, see Mirra Komarovsky, "Cultural Contradictions and Sex Roles," *American Journal of Sociology,* Vol. LII (1946), pp. 184-189.

14. Paul Wallin, "Cultural Contradictions and Sex Roles: A

Repeat Study," *American Sociological Review,* Vol. 15 (1950), pp. 288-293.

15. Kornei Tchoukovsky, *From Two to Five,* cited in K. S. Carol, "Soviet Tiny Tots," *New Statesmen,* Vol. LVII (1959), p. 568.

16. August B. Hollingshead, *Elmtown's Youth,* New York: Wiley, 1949, pp. 184, 180.

17. See especially Orville G. Brim, Jr., *Sociology and the Field of Education,* New York: Russell Sage Foundation, 1958, Chapter V; and W. Lloyd Warner, R. J. Havighurst, and M. B. Loeb, *Who Shall Be Educated?* New York: Harper, 1944. Also see Talcott Parsons, "The School Class as a Social System: Some of Its Functions in American Society," *Harvard Educational Review,* Vol. 29 (1959), pp. 297-318. In this article which centers on the classroom in the elementary school, Parsons very lucidly analyzes the importance of achievement as a criterion of selection, even in elementary school years, and shows how the teacher, through bridging the "particularistic" perspective of the family and the more "universalistic" standards of the larger society, helps to reorganize the pupil's personality. This article is a major contribution to our knowledge of socialization.

18. For a further analysis of the difference between the teacher's "universalistic" criterion of performance, and the mother's "particularistic" criterion of the individual child, see Talcott Parsons, *The Social System,* pp. 240-242.

19. W. Lloyd Warner and James C. Abegglen, *Big Business Leaders in America,* New York: Harper, 1955, p. 79.

20. Carson McGuire and George D. White, "Social Origins of Teachers—in Texas," Chapter 3 in *The Teacher's Role in American Society,* ed. Lindley J. Stiles, New York: Harper and Bros., 1957.

21. See C. Wayne Gordon, *The Social System of the High School,* Glencoe, Ill.: The Free Press, 1957; H. Otto Dahlke, *Values in Culture and Classroom,* New York: Harper, 1959; August B. Hollingshead, *op. cit.;* and James S. Coleman, "The Adolescent Subculture and Academic Achievement," *American Journal of Sociology,* Vol. LXV (1960), pp. 337-347.

22. See Lewis Yablonsky, "The Delinquent Gang as a Near-Group," *Social Problems,* Vol. VII (1959), pp. 108-117.

23. Herman R. Lantz, *op. cit.*, p. 298. The subtleties of a peer group sex code in an Italian slum district are well brought out in William F. Whyte, "A Slum Sex Code," *American Journal of Sociology*, Vol. XLIX (1943), pp. 24-31.

24. H. Otto Dahlke, *op. cit.*, p. 372.

25. Robert Dubin, "Deviant Behavior and Social Structure: Continuities in Social Theory," *American Sociological Review*, Vol. 24 (1949), p. 152.

26. W. Somerset Maugham, *Of Human Bondage*, New York: Doubleday, Doran, 1915, pp. 40-41.

27. Albert K. Cohen, *Delinquent Boys*, Glencoe, Ill.: The Free Press, 1955, pp. 27-28.

28. Carson McCullers, *The Member of the Wedding*, New York: Houghton Mifflin, 1946 (1958 Bantam edition, p. 10). By permission.

29. Clifford R. Shaw and Henry D. McKay, *Social Factors in Juvenile Delinquency*, Washington, D.C.: U.S. Government Printing Office, 1931.

30. See Dorothy Mills and M. Bishop, "Onward and Upward with the Arts: Songs of Innocence," *New Yorker*, Nov. 13, 1937, pp. 32-42; and especially Iona and Peter Opie, *The Lore and Language of School Children*, New York: Oxford University Press, 1960.

31. Allison Davis, *Social Class Influences Upon Learning*, Cambridge: Harvard University Press, 1948, p. 30.

32. William A. Westley and Frederick Elkin, "The Protective Environment and Adolescent Socialization," *Social Forces*, Vol. 35 (1957), p. 249.

33. David Riesman, *The Lonely Crowd*, New Haven: Yale University Press, 1950, pp. 70-71.

34. A recent *sociological* study of the mass media, which brings together some of the most important research in this area, is Charles R. Wright, *Mass Communication: A Sociological Perspective*, New York: Random House, 1959.

35. Faculty of Oak Lake Country Day School, "The Impact of TV," *Childhood Education*, May, 1954. Also see Hilde T. Himmelweit, A. N. Oppenheim, and Pamela Vince, *Television and the Child*, New York: Oxford University Press, 1958. That children learn the characteristics of social types is shown in the report of an experiment by Alberta E. Siegel. She presented a series of radio dramas about aggressive taxi drivers to second grade pupils and subse-

quently tested the pupils on their expectations of the behavior of real taxi drivers. "The Influence of Violence in the Mass Media upon Children's Role Expectations," *Child Development*, Vol. 29 (1958), pp. 35-56.

36. R. C. Peterson and L. L. Thurstone, *Motion Pictures and the Social Attitudes of Children*, New York: Macmillan, 1933.

37. Theodore M. Newcomb, *Social Psychology*, New York: Dryden Press, 1950, pp. 207ff.

38. Patricia L. Kendall and Katherine Wolf, "The Analysis of Deviant Cases in Communications Research," in *Communications Research 1948-49*, eds. Paul F. Lazarsfeld and F. Stanton, New York: Harper, 1949; see also Eunice Cooper and Marie Jahoda, "The Evasion of Propaganda," *Journal of Psychology*, Vol. 23 (1947), pp. 15-25.

39. Thelma McCormack, Frederick Elkin, and William A. Westley, "Anxiety and Persuasion," *Public Opinion Quarterly*, Vol. XXIII (1959), pp. 127-133.

40. The significance of mass media hero models is suggested in a study of children's reactions to two versions of a space serial; in one the leader is authoritarian and power-oriented, in the other he is friendly and affiliation-oriented. Robert B. Zajonc, "Some Effects of the 'Space' Serials," *Public Opinion Quarterly*, Vol. 18 (1954-1955), pp. 367-374.

41. Katherine M. Wolf and Marjorie Fiske, "The Children Talk About Comics," in Paul F. Lazarsfeld and F. Stanton, *op. cit.*

42. Himmelweit, Oppenheim, and Vince, *op. cit.*, Chapter 9.

43. Matilda W. Riley and John W. Riley, Jr., "A Sociological Approach to Communications Research," *Public Opinion Quarterly*, Vol. XV (1951), pp. 445-460.

44. Mildred J. Wiese and Stewart G. Cole, "A Study of Children's Attitudes and the Influence of a Commercial Motion Picture," *Journal of Psychology*, Vol. 21 (1946), pp. 151-171.

45. David Riesman, *op. cit.*, p. 77.

CHAPTER 5 *Socialization and Subcultural Patterns*

1. Celia Stendler, *Children of Brasstown*, Urbana: University of Illinois Press, 1949.

2. Bernice Neugarten, Chap. 5 in W. Lloyd Warner et al., *Democracy in Jonesville*, New York: Harper, 1949.

3. Frederick Elkin, "Harold Holzer," *Clinical Supplement to the Journal of Abnormal and Social Psychology*, Vol. 38 (1943), pp. 62, 85.

4. Cf. Alfred C. Kinsey, Wardell B. Pomeroy, and Clyde E. Martin, *Sexual Behavior in the Human Male*, Philadelphia: Saunders, 1948, Chap. 10.

5. Allison Davis, "Socialization and Adolescent Personality," *Adolescence, Forty-Third Yearbook*, Part I, Chicago: National Society for the Study of Education, 1944, Chap. II. Also see Arnold W. Green, *op. cit.*

6. Allison Davis, "The Motivation of the Underprivileged Worker," Chap. V in *Industry and Society*, ed. William F. Whyte, New York: McGraw-Hill, 1946, p. 89.

7. *Ibid.*, p. 99.

8. Roy Lewis and Angus Maude, *The English Middle Classes*, London: Penguin, 1953, p. 21.

9. A. Davis, "The Motivation of the Underprivileged Worker," p. 103.

10. Melvin L. Kohn, "Social Class and Parental Values," *American Journal of Sociology*, Vol. LXIV (1959), p. 339.

11. *Ibid.*, p. 350.

12. Joseph A. Kahl, *The American Class Structure*, New York: Rinehart, 1957, p. 249.

13. Urie Bronfenbrenner, "Socialization and Social Class Through Time and Space," in Eleanor E. Maccoby, Theodore M. Newcomb, and Eugene L. Hartley, *Readings in Social Psychology*, 3rd ed., New York: Holt, 1958, pp. 400-425.

14. *Ibid.* Also see two other well-done recent studies: Robert R. Sears, Eleanor E. Maccoby, and Harry Levin, *Patterns of Child Rearing*, Evanston, Ill.: Row, Peterson, 1957; and Donald R. Miller and Guy E. Swanson, *The Changing American Parent*, New York: Wiley, 1958.

15. Melvin L. Kohn, "Social Class and Parental Authority," *American Sociological Review*, Vol. 24 (1959), pp. 352-366.

16. For a review of several studies of mobility, see Bernard Barber, *Social Stratification*, New York: Harcourt, Brace, 1957, Chap. 16.

17. A recent study of *downwardly* mobile persons is Harold L.

Wilensky and Hugh Edwards, "The Skidder: Ideological Adjustments of Downward Mobile Workers," *American Sociological Review*, Vol. 24 (1959), pp. 215-231.

18. Richard Hoggart, *The Uses of Literacy*, London: Chatto and Windus, 1957, p. 246.

19. Among the sources not already cited which describe social class-ways of life and problems of mobility are W. Lloyd Warner and Paul S. Lunt, *The Social Life of a Modern Community*, New Haven: Yale University Press, 1941; Kurt B. Mayer, *Class and Society*, New York: Random House, 1955; James West, *Plainville, U.S.A.*, New York: Columbia University Press, 1945; Michael Yung and Peter Willmott, *Family and Kinship in East London*, London: Routledge and Kegan Paul, 1957; Allison Davis, Burleigh B. Gardner, and Mary R. Gardner, *Deep South*, Chicago: University of Chicago Press, 1941; Reinhard Bendix and Seymour M. Lipset, eds., *Status and Power: A Reader in Social Stratification*, Glencoe, Ill.: The Free Press, 1953; Allison Davis and John Dollard, *Children of Bondage*, Washington: American Council on Education, 1940. Also see Russell Lynes, "Highbrow, Lowbrow, Middlebrow," *Harper's*, February, 1949, for a half-serious discussion of social styles of life.

20. In a study of four-year-old Negro and white children in New England, Mary Ellen Goodman finds not only race awareness, but race prejudice. She shows too that the origins of racial attitudes cannot be easily explained; they derive from a complex of physical, psychological, and social factors. *Race Awareness in Young Children*, Cambridge: Addison-Wesley, 1952.

21. Marion Radke Yarrow, "Personality Development and Minority Group Membership," in *The Jews: Social Patterns of an American Group*, ed. Marshall Sklare, Glencoe, Ill.: The Free Press, 1958, pp. 455-456.

22. Elena Padilla, *Up from Puerto Rico*, New York: Columbia University Press, 1958, p. 31.

23. Toshio Yatsushiro, "The Japanese Americans," in *American Minorities*, ed. M. L. Barron, New York: Knopf, 1957, pp. 322-323.

24. Reported in Beatrice Griffith, *American Me*, New York: Houghton, Mifflin, 1948, p. 151.

25. Quoted in Irvin L. Child, *Italian or American? The Second*

Generation in Conflict, New Haven: Yale University Press, 1943, p. 105.

26. Robin M. Williams, Jr., *The Reduction of Intergroup Tensions,* New York: Social Science Research Council, 1947, p. 3.

27. Fred L. Strodtbeck, "Family Interaction, Values, and Achievement," in Marshall Sklare, *op. cit.,* p. 149.

28. Bernard C. Rosen, "Race, Ethnicity, and the Achievement Syndrome," *American Sociological Review,* Vol. 24 (1959), pp. 47-60.

29. *Ibid.*

30. Kurt Lewin, *Resolving Social Conflicts,* New York: Harper, 1948, p. 177.

31. See Herbert J. Gans, "The Origin and Growth of a Jewish Community in the Suburbs: A Study of the Jews of Park Forest, in Marshall Sklare, *op. cit.,* pp. 205-248.

32. See Will Herberg, *Protestant-Catholic-Jew,* New York: Doubleday, 1955; and Oscar Handlin, *The American People in the Twentieth Century,* Cambridge: Harvard University Press, 1954.

33. See, for example, Arthur J. Vidich and Joseph Bensman, *Small Town in Mass Society,* Princeton: Princeton University Press, 1958, Chap. 4; and Granville Hicks, *Small Town,* New York: Macmillan, 1946, pp. 200ff.

34. For an excellent study of the effect of suburban movement on the English working-class family, see Michael Young and Peter Willmott, *op. cit.*

35. Wendell Bell, "Social Choice, Life Styles, and Suburban Residence," in *The Suburban Community,* ed. William M. Dobriner, New York: Putnam, 1948, p. 231.

36. A. C. Spectorsky, *The Exurbanites,* New York: Lippincott, 1955, p. 248.

37. Walter T. Martin, "The Structuring of Social Relationships Engendered by Suburban Residence," *American Sociological Review,* Vol. 21 (1956), pp. 446-453.

38. Quoted in William H. Whyte, Jr., *The Organization Man,* New York: Doubleday, p. 378.

39. John R. Seeley, R. Alexander Sim, and E. W. Loosley, *Crestwood Heights,* New York: Basic Books, 1956, p. 277.

40. *Time,* Jan. 27, 1958, p. 38.

41. David Riesman, "The Suburban Sadness," in William M. Dobriner, *op. cit.,* pp. 376-377.

42. See William A. Westley and Frederick Elkin, *op. cit.;* and Frederick Elkin and William A. Westley, "The Myth of Adolescent Culture," *American Sociological Review,* Voı. 20 (1955), pp. 680-684.
43. William A. Westley and Frederick Elkin, *op. cit.,* p. 245.
44. Ernest R. Mowrer, "The Family in Suburbia," in William M. Dobriner, *op. cit.,* p. 156.
45. Willian. A. Westley and Frederick Elkin, *op. cit.,* p. 245.
46. Ernest R. Mowrer, *op. cıt ,* p. 156.
47. Harold L. Wattel, "Levittown: A Suburban Community," in William M. Dobriner, *op. cit.,* p. 298.
48. *Ibid.,* p. 302.

CHAPTER 6 *Socialization in Later Life*

1. Among the several studies that discuss socialization in the medical world are: Robert K. Merton, George C. Reader, and Patricia L. Kendall, *The Student Physician: Introductory Studies in the Sociology of Medical Education,* Cambridge: Harvard University Press, 1957; Talcott Parsons, *The Social System,* Glencoe, Ill.: Free Press, 1951, Chap. X; Oswald Hall, "The Informal Organization of the Medical Profession," *Canadian Journal of Economics and Political Science,* Vol. 12 (1946), pp. 30-44; and Howard S. Becker and Blanche Geer, "The Fate of Idealism in Medical School," *American Sociological Review,* Vol. 23 (1958), pp. 50-56. For an insightful analysis of the socialization ot an officer in the United States Coast Guard, see Sanford M. Dornbusch, "The Military Academy as an Assimilating Institution," *Social Forces,* Vol. 33 (1955), pp. 316-321. Everett C. Hughes has also guided considerable research on socialization into various occupations; see *American Journal of Sociology,* March, 1952.
2. Robert K. Merton and A. S. Kitt suggest the concept "anticipatory socialization" for the adoption of the values of a group to which one aspires. *Op. cit.,* pp. 87-89.
3. See Kenneth Burke, *Permanence and Change,* Los Altos, Calif.: Hermes Publications, 1954, revised edition, pp. 48-49; and Robert K. Merton, "Bureaucratic Structure and Personality," *Social Forces,* Vol. 17 (1940), pp. 560-568.
4. See Charles H. Page, "Bureaucracy's Other Face," *Social Forces,* Vol. 25 (1946), pp. 88-94.

5. David Riesman and Howard E. Roseborough have given the term "retroactive socialization" to the process by which the older generation learns from the younger. "Careers and Consumer Behavior," Chap. I in Lincoln H. Clark, *Consumer Behavior,* New York: New York University Press, 1955.

SELECTED READINGS

Barker, Roger G., and Herbert F. Wright, *Midwest and Its Children,* Evanston, Ill.: Row Peterson and Co., 1956.
    The authors present detailed information on the everyday lives and behavior settings of the children in a small midwestern town.

Bossard, James H. S. and Eleanor S. Boll, *The Sociology of Child Development,* New York: Harper & Bros., 3rd Ed., 1960.
    This textbook brings together much of the research in sociology relating to children and introduces some suggestive material on routines of family life.

Cohen, Albert K., *Delinquent Boys: The Culture of the Gang,* Glencoe, Ill.: The Free Press, 1955.
    The author presents a theory of the "delinquent subculture," relating it to the frustrations of the working-class child and the pressures of middle-class standards which he is ill-equipped to meet.

Erikson, Erik H., *Childhood and Society,* New York: W. W. Norton & Co., 1950.
    Erikson employs a modified psychoanalytic approach in discussing stages of development and in analyzing the relationship between childhood training and cultural characteristics.

Hollingshead, August B., *Elmtown's Youth,* New York: John Wiley and Sons, 1949.

This is a study of the behavior patterns of adolescents in a small city in Illinois, placed in the framework of the social class structure.

Josselyn, Irene M., *The Happy Child,* New York: Random House, 1955.
The author presents a clear and simple analysis of the development of the child from a psychoanalytic point of view.

Lindesmith, Alfred R., and Anselm L. Strauss, *Social Psychology,* New York: The Dryden Press, Rev. ed., 1956.
In analyzing social relationships from a "symbolic interactionist" point of view, the authors follow many of the ideas of George H. Mead.

McCullers, Carson, *The Member of the Wedding,* New York: Houghton Mifflin Co., 1946.
This novel, subsequently made into a play and film, sensitively portrays the feelings of a twelve-year-old girl who feels there is no group in the world to which she belongs.

Mead, Margaret, and Martha Wolfenstein, eds., *Childhood in Contemporary Cultures,* Chicago: University of Chicago Press, 1955.
The orientation of this series of studies is cultural and psychoanalytic. The sources include direct observation, novels about children, and children's art.

Parsons, Talcott, and Robert F. Bales, *Family, Socialization and Interaction Process,* Glencoe, Ill.: The Free Press, 1955.
Parsons and his colleagues apply his theoretical framework for the analysis of the "social system" to the family. This is a further development of his chapter on socialization in *The Social System,* Glencoe, Ill.: The Free Press, 1951.

Piaget, Jean, *The Language and Thought of the Child,* London: Routledge and Kegan Paul Ltd., Rev. ed., 1932.
Any of Piaget's books indicate his approach and his method. This is one of his earliest and most significant.

Riesman, David, *The Lonely Crowd,* New Haven: Yale University Press, 1950.

The author refers to many agencies of socialization to illustrate his thesis that there is a trend in our society from "inner-" to "other-direction."

Salinger, J. D., *The Catcher in the Rye,* Boston: Little, Brown & Co., 1951.

The hero of this novel is a sixteen-year-old boy who is seeking rather desperately to crystallize his image of himself and the surrounding world.

Sarbin, Theodore R., "Role Theory," in *Handbook of Social Psychology,* Vol. I, ed. Gardner Lindzey, Cambridge, Mass.: Addison-Wesley, 1954, pp. 223-258.

The author presents a theory of role behavior with particular emphasis on experiments which illustrate and support the theory.

Sears, Robert R., Eleanor E. Maccoby, and Harry Levin, *Patterns of Child Rearing,* Evanston, Ill.: Row, Peterson and Co., 1957.

Using an interview schedule to collect information, the authors have carefully and intensively studied the child-rearing patterns of 379 families in the Boston area.

Seeley, John R., R. Alexander Sim, and E. W. Loosley, *Crestwood Heights,* New York: Basic Books Inc., 1956.

This is a study of a well-to-do suburb in Canada whose primary concern is the rearing of children.

Spiro, Melford E., *Children of the Kibbutz,* Cambridge: Harvard University Press, 1958.

This is a report of a fascinating social experiment. In this Israeli kibbutz, children are reared under a system of collective education; they do not live with their parents and parents have little authority over them.

Strauss, Anselm, ed., *The Social Psychology of George Herbert Mead,* Chicago: University of Chicago Press, 1956.

This volume consists of selections from the writings of Mead, focusing on his social psychology.

Whyte, William F., *Street Corner Society,* Chicago: University of Chicago Press, 2nd ed., 1955.

This is a study of the social structure of an Italian slum

area during the depression, with particular attention devoted to the life of the "corner boys."

Wright, Richard, *Black Boy,* New York: Harper & Bros., 1937.
This autobiography is slanted and dated, but it is still a
most perceptive and dramatic account of a Negro boyhood.